GETTING IT, THEN GETTING ALONG

....

Understanding the
world's five major religions:
COLLABORATIVE RATHER THAN DIVISIVE

....

L. REYNOLDS ANDIRIC, Ed D

Copyright: Linda R. Andiric

Print ISBN: 978-1-54399-117-8

eBook ISBN: 978-1-54399-118-5

Library of Congress Control Number:

Printed in the USA

TABLE OF CONTENTS

IMPORTANT TO read!

My goal in writing this book is for the reader to learn about five major religious paths that are practiced by a majority of peoples in the world today—most likely because of their heritage and/or place of birth. If, after gaining a broader insight into each of the spiritual practices, the outcome is a better understanding of the religious beliefs of others, I have achieved my mission. Greater understanding will hopefully translate not only into respect for others' beliefs, but religious diversity may even be valued.

The earth is large enough to accommodate us all, regardless of our different perspectives and ideologies. Ultimately this acceptance and respect for our different ideologies might save our planet and all of us together may be able to resolve our greatest threats.

Please consider carefully the information and explanations in the interim chapters describing the five major religions and seek to walk momentarily in the shoes of others who follow each path. Try to develop empathy for them. The worth of any book is to change the reader for the better in some small way. My aim for this book is to help halt the violence against others by fostering understanding in reference to their spiritual beliefs. The reader is encouraged to regard our differences with a positive attitude and consider that the sum of our beliefs might be truly greater than our individual philosophies and together as a global community, we can work together to find solutions needed by all. As a result, our planet could be free of war, disease and the misuse of nature. If this can work for religion, it can also work for race, gender, politics or any of the things that divide us.

L. Reynolds Andiric

My sincere thanks also to: Sally Ryden, Ghada Chatila, Phyllis Bransky, Marie and Jim Akers for their valuable suggestions and critiques of this manuscript.

Dear Reader,

When I was five years old, I went to Sunday school and listened as my teacher read stories from both the Old and New Testament. My mother also read them to me from a Bible storybook that had pictures of Noah and pairs of animals marching to the ark; or baby Jesus in the manger; or Jesus with fishermen, and Jesus with small children. The illustrations in the book were very colorful and remain embedded in my memory.

But some were also scary. For example, Abraham was poised with a huge dagger to murder his own son. I didn't understand God at all in regard to that one. Not many could pass that test! In Sunday school, after the teacher finished reading, we had a picture to color relating to the story we had just heard. Sometimes we had a Bible verse to remember and we would usually sing a song or two. I felt happy and pleased with my Sunday school experiences. I liked to color, and it was a joyful time with the other children in my class. The pictures were meaningful to me since we had just heard a story about them, and I liked to imagine how my picture related to the story.

I was about ten years old when I attended an evening special service at our church with my parents. The guest speaker talked about the New Testament scripture that stated that Jesus said, "For God so loved the world that he gave his one and only Son, that whoever believes in him shall not perish but have eternal life" (John 3:16). The speaker emphasized that Jesus was the only way to salvation and if we didn't accept him and believe that to be true, we would be lost to God. I liked Jesus, so my first thoughts were that this posed no problem for me. Then from the audience, the question arose: What if someone had never heard of Jesus? What if they lived very far away in the deepest darkest part of Africa or in the Amazon jungle? Were they lost to God? Were they dammed and not saved? That then, really began to upset me as I listened to the message that unless one believed in Jesus, they were excluded from salvation and would not be able to get into heaven! How could God be so mean, I asked myself? If a person never heard of Jesus, how could they be blamed and then punished for it?

I didn't ponder this a lot afterward, but from time to time when I remembered this admonition, I found it difficult to fathom a god with such unfair and biased rules. But church was an important part of my life; it was our family's Sunday routine, and when I became a teenager, I became further involved with the church's youth group. It was at a youth meeting when I was sixteen that I had my first and only charismatic religious experience. It was strange and enigmatic. I had never felt such excitement and exhilaration as my heart began to beat rapidly and I felt like I was radiating energy and light. I wanted to laugh and cry at the same time. I felt hot and chilled simultaneously.

We spent a week at a youth conference at a Presbyterian College in Muskegon, Ohio and it was during the final closing candlelight ceremony that I had this most unforgettable experience. Approximately 500 youths were in attendance and each of us had been given a candle, which was lit while we walked in a procession from the chapel service, downhill to a meeting place on the moonlit lakefront. It was during this processional that my strange physiological feelings occurred.

As I looked ahead at the lights from the candles carried by the youths now hidden by the darkness of night, the flickering candles serpentined ahead along the trail as far as I could see. We walked silently and the experience profoundly affected me both physiologically and spiritually as I felt in those few minutes a union with all life but especially my youthful cohort. I have never forgotten the beautiful scene it portrayed and the exhilarating feelings I experienced. When I hear of persons having a "born again" occurrence or when people say Jesus talks to them, I never discount those accounts because I, too, have witnessed and felt a mystical event that has stayed with me all my life. To again feel that unity with all that exists is my strong desire.

As an adult, my path in life has taken me to many parts of the world and I've been lucky that I have been able to observe and befriend many persons from different cultures who have strikingly different religious beliefs than those of my childhood. I'm convinced that, for the most part, people's beliefs are mostly influenced by their heritage, their culture, and how they are taught within that framework.

In other words, if I'd been born in a Muslim country, I would most likely experience my religiosity as conveyed in the Quran because that would be my sole frame of reference. If my immediate family was devout and more demonstrative in their religious practice, I would most likely be more fervent, also. If their practices were less important to them, they would probably not be a priority for me either unless I was old enough to acquire my own religious thoughts and experiences.

A question I've often reflected on is why so many, who have their own quite fundamental beliefs and literal interpretation of their chosen ideology, seem to demand that everyone agree exclusively with their specific philosophy. When in my childhood, the speaker at our Methodist church opined that unless one accepted Jesus as their savior they would be doomed; the message I received was a negative one.

That desperate choice could be the impetus for why many believers are so insistent to spread their doctrine. They feel compelled to save us all from the alleged tragedy of being "lost". At first glance, this might be considered to be both generous and unselfish by those who are concerned for our welfare. However, it can become judgmental, unwelcome, and hurtful. Instead of presenting a choice to be considered, it disregards another traditional Christian doctrine, that of free will.

Within each individual is a different heritage, including a uniquely developed intellect influenced by a variety of experiences that ultimately results in an individual viewpoint that defines our specific personal religious beliefs. Just as each person has a different physical appearance, it's reasonable to expect that each individual will acquire their own understanding, attitude and feeling regarding their personal spirituality. Each is at a different place on the continuum of spirituality that has evolved from their heritage, their experiences, their intellect, their spiritual understanding and interests. Additionally, if one believes in the concept of reincarnation, those things learned in other lifetimes will add more experiences to the emotional, intellectual, and spiritual viewpoint.

For peace to be possible, we must acknowledge that we are each on our own divine path of spirituality that has evolved specifically for and by each individual. Furthermore, our attitudes are most likely defined by the capabilities we possess at this moment or any given future moment. Although the ardent concern for other souls (by those who have the belief that we must all follow their ideology) is indeed intended with the greatest of sincerity, enthusiasts need to be cognizant that others may have different concepts for spiritual practice and they should be respected.

Peaceful acceptance of others' beliefs is really quite simple then; each must allow and facilitate, but not dictate or cajole others to walk a certain path. We must all walk our own path to find the way to our individual destination.

L. Reynolds Andiric

WHERE WE ARE

This is *not* a book about religious doctrine or dogma. The purpose of this book is not to convince the reader that any one belief system is better than another, or to convert the reader to any one religious philosophy. The intent, rather, is to inform what the beliefs of the five major religions are, their origins, and how they have evolved into what they are today. It should be remembered that there are many other belief systems also—not only the five major ones that will be discussed here. With better understanding, we might recognize the things that unite us and come to respect the things that divide us.

Following 9/11 and continuing throughout the United States today, there has been a surge of violence toward Muslims and those mistaken for Muslims. For example, the *Sikhs*, a group of people who emigrated from the Punjab Province in India to America, have endured much aggression. They are not Muslim at all but are a religious community who are followers of the 16th century Guru Nanak who rejected the elaborate rituals of Hinduism, but stressed the importance of service to others, doing good deeds and treating every person equally with kindness and respect.

Sikh men don't cut their hair. They wear turbans, and grow beards. There are twenty-five million Sikh followers worldwide; 500,000 in the United States who are hard-working citizens and typically feel grateful to the U. S. for providing them a means to achieve

the American dream. Often mistaken as Muslim, they have been tar-
geted since 9/11 in hundreds of crimes including shootings.

A doctor/professor walking in Central Park in New York City
was attacked and severely beaten by boys shouting, "Terrorist Osama,
get him!" Those wanting to kill "towel heads" gunned down a Sikh
who was getting into his car in the driveway of his home. Another was
shot at his gas station business. Most notable perhaps, was a mass
shooting during a Sunday service in Milwaukee, Wisconsin by a white
supremacist who killed six and injured four.

Yet, the frequent response from those whose lives have been
touched with such violence has not been revenge, but the hope that
attackers will be educated and have their "hearts awakened".

Multiple reports surfaced around 2005 regarding U. S. military
prison guards and interrogators who intentionally desecrated both
Muslims and the Quran, the holy book of Islam. One Muslim detainee
was photographed being led around with a dog collar and leash. From
Guantanamo Bay to Abu Ghraib and prisons throughout Afghanistan
and Iraq, reports of "urinating" on the Quran or throwing the book
into the toilet surfaced through official channels and were reported to
the world by Newsweek and other media sources. The response from
some Muslims was massive and violent.

Throughout the world, in fact, religion-sourced atrocities continue today. In Myanmar, a minority group of Muslims, the Rohingya,
who have lived in the Rakhine state of the Buddhist-majority country for generations, are not recognized as citizens by the Myanmar
government. The Rohingya are restricted from moving about in
Myanmar, they are deprived of a livelihood, and have no rights to

health care, education, or to practice their religion. Myanmar security forces continually harass them. Tensions have resulted not only in mass killings, but there are accusations of potential genocide perpetuated by the nationalistic Buddhist majority. A mass exodus across the border into Bangladesh by the Rohingya has overwhelmed that country resulting in insufficient food and shelter.

Because the Myanmar government is no longer led by the military, it might logically follow that the government would have tremendous influence to curb the violence and to recognize the Rohingya's right to citizenship and protection. The government, and its Nobel Peace Prize leader Aung San Suu Kyi, have not yet addressed the situation and claim it doesn't exist.

These are but a few of the hundreds of violent occurrences around the world in recent times. It is a fact of our human history that one group or another has been attacked simply because of who they are and what group they have descended from.

Most notably Jews, but often Christians, have been ousted and exterminated throughout history because of their beliefs. All too often, another violent hate-crime or shooting is reported, sometimes within days or weeks of the previous one.

Attacks by white supremacists and revenge attacks by radicalized Islamic terrorists include the bombing of little girls who were accompanied by their mothers at an Ariana Grande music concert in Manchester, England; a mass shooting during a bible study group in Charleston, S. C.; a shooting during a Passover service in a synagogue in Poway, California. Violence against "others" has become a too-frequent event—many times allegedly carried out for "religious" reasons by "religious" people.

Because many of the conflicts throughout history, as well as around the globe today have, at their source, the intolerance of religious beliefs and practices, it is hoped that by examining others' practices a little more closely, we might see there's much in common.

A powerful realization is that the major religious philosophies are followed based on where in the world, and into what culture an individual was born and raised.

Could such awareness lead to a more peaceful, tolerant coexistence? If so, even a small step in that direction would be a far cry from the world of today that is fraught with divisiveness, suspicion, mistrust and violence.

Throughout history, accurate information, education and truth have often resolved misunderstandings. A problem today in our instantaneous "breaking news" culture resulting in "instant outrage" is that propaganda is often presented and alleged to be factual without corroboration. Social media posts often originate from opinion and then unsubstantiated perpetuation of false information occurs to justify a particular viewpoint or agenda.

We might even consider that misinformation and ignorance are reinforced daily and *they* are the real enemies. In recognizing this, we must be open to having our own socially-sourced opinions challenged, updated or even changed, and if we're truly committed to living in peace, it's up to us, our decision, to be sincere and open-minded in the search for real truth—not settling for or accepting the opinions and statements spread throughout the world via Twitter and Facebook.

The content of this book's following chapters focuses on five major religions of the world. The information has been researched, read, amended and further clarified or modified by a learned, knowledgeable practitioner from within each of those religions.

The resulting explanations are not meant to be scholarly, theological or of a dogmatic nature that is painstakingly detailed, but rather, they are meant to provide a comprehensive but easily understandable summary of that religion's origin and evolution and a clear and simple description of what and how someone of this faith practices their beliefs.

My intention is to provide and promote more understanding and a tolerant attitude toward the "others" who practice their religious beliefs differently from mine—or yours.

His Holiness the Dali Lama is credited with saying that it doesn't matter if a person is religious or not; more important is that they are a good human being (Dali Lama, Ed: Mehotra, 2006). We are indeed human beings first and foremost, having evolved, hopefully, from a more primitive state of "feed, flight, fight and reproduce." Our human brains have developed a cortex capable of replacing basic, primitive actions and reactions with thought and more refined behaviors.

Yet in regard to another's beliefs - especially other's *religious* beliefs—for many there is only one way—*their* way. This attitude promotes a separatist way of thinking rather than an attitude of openness and tolerance and often results in the position that I, alone, know the truth and therefore anyone who doesn't believe as I do is simply *wrong*. Many times, it also follows, that the separatist feels it's their *duty* to reveal their interpretation of the *truth* and with that, a righteous indignation often develops, which may include violence.

As the orthodox Jewish scholar and former Chief Rabbi of the United Kingdom, Rabbi Jonathan Sacks, so ably stated: "We need to understand that just as the natural environment depends on biodiversity, so the human environment depends on cultural diversity, because no one civilization encompasses all the spiritual, ethical and artistic expressions of mankind." (Sacks, 2000.)

Taking this only one small step further, it's helpful to realize that when two ideas conflict, it doesn't necessarily follow that one is true, and the other is false. Rather, it might be that there is a different perspective or point of view often brought about by one's culture and environment—including their life experiences.

Certainly, if we are born into a certain culture, we will generally adopt the native, inherited belief system within that culture. Furthermore, the degree to which any belief system is practiced is wholly dependent upon the circumstances an individual finds him or herself in. It is perhaps possible and even relevant to understand that every culture has something to contribute to the human condition and although we may not have shared the exact same experiences or we may not think exactly alike, we might learn from one another and, at the very least, develop an understanding and respect for each other's ways of thinking and beliefs.

Or, perhaps by combining our knowledge and experiences, a more complete truth can be realized where the sum of our knowledge is greater than any individual information. Together, our contributions can build something bigger than we could experience separately.

The Abrahamic religions are a major source of conflict in many places throughout the world, but particularly in the Middle East. Perhaps, rather than thinking about them as three separate religious philosophies, they could be viewed as one philosophy that has evolved differently to be relevant and applicable to three different cultures during three different historical eras.

The first to be "chosen" were the Hebrew people, through Abraham, who formed a relationship with the one monotheistic God. A God who loved, actively assisted, and even rescued his people from slavery and servitude in a foreign land while subsequently reminding them to "be kind to the alien, as you were once aliens too." (Exodus 22:21; Leviticus 19:34, The New International Version) After some time however, the Israelites turned away from that God and his commandments, and reverted to their previous pagan gods.

Thereafter, a new covenant came about, another opportunity for peace, through Jesus who was sent to clarify, by example, how people should live and conduct their lives—not only for the Israelites (who reject this role of Jesus) but also to include the Gentiles. The visions and prophesy of Isaiah attest to this—that whosoever follows the path of God's righteousness will be accepted as God's people. Isaiah 56:6-8 states: "And foreigners who bind themselves to the Lord to serve him, all who keep the Sabbath without desecrating it and who hold fast to my covenant—these I will bring to my holy mountain and give them joy in my house of prayer. Their burnt offerings and sacrifices will be accepted on my altar for my house will be called a house of prayer for all nations".

The Sovereign Lord further declares (Jeremiah 31:33-34): "This is the covenant I will make with the house of Israel after that time [time of dispersion of Jews throughout the world] declares the Lord. I will put my law in their minds and write it on their hearts, I will be their God and they will be my people.... For I will forgive their wickedness and will remember their sins no more."

Eventually, the peoples of the desert were also included with the "chosen" as God revealed a third and final message through the Prophet Mohammad, reiterating and verifying what came before. ((Quran) Surah 5:48): "To you We sent the Scripture in truth, *confirming the scripture that came before it*, and guarding it in safety: so judge between them and what God has revealed, and do not follow their vain desires, diverging from the truth that has come to you. To each among you, We have prescribed a Law and an Open Way. If God had so willed, He would have made you a single people, but (His Plan is) to test you in what He has given you: so strive as in a race in all virtues. The goal of you all is to God; it is He that will show you the truth of the matters in which you dispute."

A major component of all three of these covenants (Jewish, Christian and Islam) is the directive to treat others with compassion and respect, as you would want to be treated. This is referred to as the so-called "Golden Rule" in Christianity, but equally present in all of the Abrahamic religious philosophies. This directive is readily accepted, but one, which history can testify to, that is not practiced when circumstances become oppressive or when disagreements and hostilities develop.

History is full of examples of suppression and violence that have resulted from distain for the "other"—those who are unlike us and do not share our beliefs. They may be viewed as less "civilized" than we are, based on their physical appearance, intelligence, or simply their refusal to believe our way. From this intolerance has spawned not only colonialism, but such atrocities as the Crusades, the genocide demonstrated during the Holocaust, the carnage of the Khmer Rouge, the massacres in Armenia, Kosovo, Rwanda and Sudan, just to name a few.

The violence during Ireland's Protestant-Catholic conflict, the South African apartheid experience of black versus white, and the present-day Taliban, ISIS, and other terrorist groups, were all based on the belief that there was only one way to please God. Any and all deviation from that "way" was met with fierce retribution.

It is important to remember that above all delineations of identity; man is first and foremost part of humanity. David Fawley (2008), a Hindu, explains it beautifully. "The oneness of the ocean exists at its depth, not at the level of the waves, which must remain ever-changing." Mankind is said to be equal in the sight of God, and even when one views existence from a purely secular perspective rather than a theological one, all beings have common psychological as well as physiological needs such as food, water, and relief from pain and conflict.

Therefore, as members of humanity we are all deserving of, at a minimum, tolerance, respect and compassion. Compassion does not mean pity, but rather imagining oneself in the other's situation and from their perspective. How would it be to deal with their problems? In other words, to adopt that omnipresent directive within every religion and civilization—to treat others, as we would want to be treated ourselves.

Karen Armstrong, a Catholic nun who left the convent after seven years, has researched, studied and written numerous scholarly books on religion. She is also the recipient of the 2008 TED Prize of one million dollars with which a desired wish of hers has become a reality. Ms Armstrong's Charter for Compassion and its twelve-step plan lays out a formalized scheme to develop and achieve compassion, encouraging everyone to examine closely how others are treated and how they themselves treat those with whom they come in contact in daily life. In her book, *Twelve Steps to a Compassionate Life*, (Armstrong, 2011) the importance of compassion for others is found to be inclusive in the philosophies of every major belief system and again we are reminded of the one basic underpinning that is present in all theologies: "Do not do to others what you wouldn't want done to you." If all followed this simple, clear statement, countries would not be invaded, possessions would not be stolen, there would be no killing, and everyone's beliefs would be respected.

The formalized plan for compassionate living that Ms. Armstrong not only promotes but also provides a charter for, requests that individuals commit to the betterment of mankind not only with respect and tolerance for our differences, but with empathy that will foster an understanding of the obstacles many face in their day-to-day existence. We are, after all, humans first. The other descriptors or labels that contribute to who we are, are secondary to our humanity.

The systematic plan contained within Armstrong's book provides a charter for an individual's compassionate living and it requires agreement that a better world is needed, and it should be every individual's goal to alleviate today's troubled world, which is certainly *not* inclusive or fair to all peoples.

The unequal treatment for many should be acknowledged with the commitment by each and every person to not only recognize this fact, but commit to do whatever small things we can to make this a better world for everyone.

Mother Teresa (n.d.) so humbly stated, "We can rarely do great things; but we can do small things with great love." A multitude of small loving and compassionate things done by many people CAN create a great change.

Attempting to understand another's beliefs without the strife and turmoil that often accompanies different viewpoints would be a small step individually and a positive step overall for the betterment of humanity. Likewise, rather than ignoring another's poor treatment and thereby allowing and even perpetuating inequality and mistreatment, we might strive not only to *understand* another's religious views and social traditions, but also to *help others* understand, and to challenge them to imagine how it would be to walk the path of those they are mistreating.

The Compassionate Living Charter suggests that the first order of business is for everyone to acknowledge that we must treat our fellow beings more respectfully if we want to achieve a better world. Furthermore, it is up to *each* of us to begin to create a better world. To summarize the thought process for a more compassionate way of life, twelve steps of self-reflection are suggested:

1. *Learn about compassion.* As previously mentioned, compassion is a tenet in all of the major religions and Ms. Armstrong (2011) describes it in detail in her book. The peoples of the world were dispersed and formed separate cultures with different beliefs, which might in fact, be God's plan. The purpose of that plan may be for us to figure out how to accept and live with those who are not like us. Rather than a passion to have things "our way", perhaps a passion for empathy and compassion are the important tools to understanding and that others have a right to "their way" as well. This requires a willingness to learn about other ways instead of automatically discounting them—to learn to accept our differences and live together in peace.

2. *Look at our own daily world.* Examine the conflicts within our own families and notice how even in this microenvironment, things can be seen and interpreted quite differently. Then look out into the community, the state, and finally the nation, for opportunities to try to understand others' points of view.

3. *Have compassion for oneself.* Accept the fact that we are not perfect beings that have the complete knowledge necessary to correctly assess every situation. We can, however, examine our thoughts, understand our weaknesses and gaps, and be open to learning what is needed to live peacefully with others, even those with a different point of view.

4. *Develop empathy*. This is where we walk a mile in someone else's shoes. With the knowledge of another's background and how it has shaped that person's thoughts and actions, we should try to imagine how, in like circumstances with the same history and background, we might act. We should endeavor to react in a positive way, rather than lashing out with insults or mistreatment.

5. *Be mindful*. Mindfulness is the trait cherished by the Buddhists as a way to live a more fulfilled life. To be mindful means that we are living in the present moment. We aren't living in the past or projecting to the future. Living in the moment allows us to put full attention on any given situation or circumstance and decide purposefully how to act or react. The past is irrelevant to today's present situation and our reaction to it. Therefore, so that the future is not burdened with regret, it is important to give full attention to how each and every interchange at *this* very moment is handled. Do we handle it with consideration and patience, or do we rush to judgment and react with hurtful actions? We should carefully and cautiously consider how to respond in every situation. This is not to say we must always agree, but we must always be cognizant that the way we respond to a discussion or situation can escalate discord or deescalate conflict if we promote respectful and useful dialogue.

6. *Take action*. Just as we cannot learn to drive a car or learn to swim by reading a book or talking about it, we must take action and become involved and practice our intentions in order to develop more compassionate behavior. This starts

at home with our family and extends outward to friends and acquaintances. Rather than reacting to a statement or action, a thoughtful response offered with respect and empathy for the other person is the preferred reaction.

7. *Recognize that ignorance is universal* and that we all face unknown situations and knowledge voids on a daily basis. We cannot know everything, particularly if there has been no prior experience with it or we know little about a given topic. We should not expound without sufficient knowledge or with only the "fake" or trumped up news that is prevalent today in the social news media whose mission is to distort the real story in order to gain converts for a specific agenda. It is better to defer an opinion until factual information can be obtained, and even then, to remain open to exploring and expanding on the truth.

8. *Develop civil discourse.* Words can do long-term damage and if the truth be known, are probably at the root of most, if not all, confrontations and volatile situations. We should there-fore be judicious and take care how we say things. We should listen to others. We don't have to agree, but common cour-tesy, rather than the degradation of the other's view, should be the norm. Some Native Americans have developed a way to achieve good communication. They involve a "talking stick" when disputes are handled, or an important decision is to be made. Each speaker is given the talking stick and with that stick in hand, expresses his viewpoint fully. No one speaks until the talking stick is passed to them, which prevents interruptions and over-talking of the speaker. The

speaker is allotted time enough to adequately explain his position. For debate, the talking stick is passed to subsequent speakers and back to the original speaker for clarification or comment if necessary. Everyone has the opportunity to speak and be part of the debate until a decision is made or a resolution is agreed upon. Each speaker explains his position or doubts regarding the proposition in a thoughtful, respectful manner without accusations, bad language or insults.

9. *Develop a concern for everybody, everywhere.* Today, the events of the world have the capacity to affect our everyday lives immensely. We should have compassion for those who are suffering around the world, those who may be restricted from truth by ruthless dictatorships or renegade gangs that overpower the weak in order to force their way for their own benefit. There are many that are misguided either by selfish intent or simply by ignorance. We must foster empathy and compassion for those caught in such situations and, if the opportunity presents itself, help them escape from it or, at least, ease their way.

10. *Educate oneself and gain knowledge.* Only by seeking the truth through accurate information about any given subject or situation can we know how to respond and speak intelligently. This does not include the opinions stated on social media or Twitter where opinions can be passed along as fact, most of the time without verification of their validity. Before we decide what to believe or what position to take, we should learn all sides of the debate to discern, as much as humanly

possible, what the truth is. This can be a lengthy exercise to be certain, but an important one that can prevent a lot of damage from inaccurate information and the ramifications that can result from that inaccurate information.

11. *Recognize that wrongs do and will occur*. This is not a perfect world, and everyone is not dedicated to acquiring accurate information. There is greed, and with greed often comes the bullying of others who are weaker. There is ignorance and often a lack of fortitude in finding the facts and the truth behind controversial topics and current events. We must do our best to assure our own ignorance is dispelled. Winning others to this realization, one by one, can be the way in which truth will win over ignorance and promote a more peaceful way of living.

12. *Love your enemies* and realize that much bad behavior stems from ignorance and intolerance of differences rather than from malevolent intent. It is said, that by keeping our enemies close, we can better understand them and prevent the negative consequences of their behavior. This practice was proven with organizations such as the Ku Klux Klan, which was successfully infiltrated and exposed. Eventually this resulted in the elimination of many of their followers.

His Holiness the Dali Lama (1998) teaches that having those in our lives with whom we disagree and dislike provides us an opportunity to practice loving kindness and respect, not to adopt the enemies' viewpoint or practices, but to understand them better and perhaps be a factor in providing information that will dispel harmful behavior on their part. Such was the case with Malcolm X (Haley, 2015), who initially had no tolerance for whites and called for their demise until he had a different experience at the Muslim hajj where white pilgrims accepted him as an equal (unlike his experience at home in the U.S.). He returned from the hajj with the realization that through education, instead of advocating for the destruction of whites, racial prejudice in the U. S. could be lessened by the elimination of ignorance and perhaps, someday, eradicated.

Mahatma Gandhi (Gandhi, 1913) advocated that as individuals, we (ourselves) must become the change we want to see in the world and it doesn't come by bullying others. That, in essence, is what I hope to invoke and provide for the reader of this book. If we can have compassion for one another and refuse to automatically discount a different position or perspective, together, we can find solutions to the injustices and turmoil in our world.

But harmony in this aspect, will take all of us attempting to live in this way. Finding truth will become a collaborative pursuit where all of our efforts and contributions finally unveil and provide understanding for a way to live together peacefully and with respect—even if it is one tiny step at a time.

A Word about Orientalism

It is imperative that I caution readers, that especially when learning about cultures quite different from their own, that they do NOT interpret another's beliefs, including the historical events that are the underpinning of those beliefs, with the perspective of their own native culture, language and ideological values.

There are, in other words, our own culture and values, and other cultures and values that may be somewhat or even vastly different— possibly even polar opposite. Because our perspectives may differ, the lens through which we view others may be distorted and therefore inaccurate by our own culture, history, and beliefs. This can promote the tendency to view the "other" as unenlightened—even ignorant, but that judgment is of no value when seeking understanding.

So it is with the Middle East and their religious and cultural beliefs, which are uniquely relevant to them including a history and environment that is embedded in their psyche and worldview. The history, beliefs, and experiences of the East (the so-called Orient) and the Western European understanding of those beliefs and experiences are often not in sync with one another and in fact might render an attitude of superiority of the western view over the eastern experience.

Those who study and interpret others' beliefs and the historical background from which those beliefs evolved, may quite naturally and unconsciously impose their own perspectives and values in their interpretations. This is unavoidable. Language and translation from one language to another may be factors as well in how we ultimately view others.

Particularly in eastern languages, including Arabic, an exact meaning may not be precisely translatable, and one must settle for the closest understanding, which may alter the true meaning. Thus, the way a westerner thinks, writes, and talks about the Orient is a matter of perspective. This understandably can pose obstacles that may result in misunderstandings and perhaps even a denigration of the other who may exhibit behavior interpreted to be counter to western thought. This challenge is all about interpretations and how different perspectives affect them.

Therefore, scholarly explanation can be one-sided as cultural events and history of the eastern experiences are interpreted from the values and perspective of the westerner. Often the conclusions reached are the opinions and thoughts of the western scholar rather than that of the others' culture. An inaccurate understanding may develop because of the problems inherent with translation. This is referred to as Orientalism whereby another's cultural heritage is interpreted and even judged by the values and cultural heritage from an observer's quite-different lens (Said, 1978).

References/Bibliography

Holy Bible: New International Version

Quran: Dawood, N. J. 1956. The Koran. Great Britain. Penguin Books.

Quran: Pickthall, M. M. (trans.) The meaning of the glorious Koran. Twelfth Printing. New York: Mentor Books.

Armstrong, K. (2011). Twelve steps to a compassionate life. New York: Anchor Books.

Basu, M. (2016). "15 years after 9/11. Sikhs still victims of anti-Muslim hate crimes." CNN. Retrieved February 2, 2017, from http://www.cnn. com/2016/09/15/us/sikh-hate-crime-victims/index.html.

Editorial Board (2016). "Evidence of Prisoner Abuse, Still Hidden." New York Times. Retrieved February 8, 2017, from http://www. Newyorktimes/AbuGhraib/html.

Fawley, D. (2008). Hinduism, the eternal tradition. New Dehli: Pub. Voice of India.

Gandhi, M. (1913). Retrieved May 8, 2019, from https://quoteinvestigator. com/2017/10/23/be-the-change/.

Haley, A. (2015). Malcolm X. New York: Ballantine Books.

Haltiwanger, J. (2017). "Is genocide occurring against the Rohingya in Myanmar?" Newsweek. Retrieved on September 26, 2017, from https:www.newsweek.com/genocide-occurring against-rohingya-myanmar/html.

Hilal, M. (2017). "Abu Ghraib: The legacy of torture in the war on terror." Aljazeera.

Retrieved on February 8, 2017, from https://www.aljazeera.com/indepth/ opinion/abu-ghraib-legacy-torture-war-terror-170928154012053. html.

Jayaram, V. "Sikhism, basic concepts." (n.d.). Retrieved February 2, 2017, from http://www.hinduwebsite.com/sikhism/glossary.asp.

Mehotra, R. (Ed.). (2005). *The essential Dalai Lama: His important teachings.* New York: Penguin Books.

Mother Teresa. (2007). *Love: The words and inspiration of Mother Teresa.* Blue Mountain Arts.

Paul, D. & Mettler, K. (2019). "Authorities identify suspect in 'hate crime' synagogue Shooting that left 1 dead, 3 injured." *Washington Post.* Retrieved April 28, 2019, from https://www.washingtonpost.com/.../04.../california-synagogue- shooting.html.

Said, E. W. (1978). *Orientalism.* New York: Pantheon Books.

Sacks, J. (2000). *The dignity of difference: How to avoid the clash of civilizations.* New York: Continuum.

Shapiro, E. (2015). "Key moments in Charleston church shooting case a Dylann Roof Pleads guilty." *ABC News.* Retrieved June 20, 2017, from https://abcnews.go.com/alerts/charleston-shooting.html.

Smith, R. & Chan, S. (2017). "Ariana Grande Manchester concert ends in explosion, panic and death." *The New York Times.* Retrieved January 18, 2018, from https://www.nytimes.com/2017/05/22/world/.../ariana-grande-manchester-police.html.

JUDAISM

History

The great flood of which Noah is said to have saved a male and female specimen of every species of all creatures is estimated to have occurred around 2105 BCE (Hebrew Calendar). The descendants of Noah's sons, within several generations, spread out over the earth yet all spoke a common language.

"Then, they said, 'Come, let's build ourselves a city, with a tower that reaches to the heavens, so that we may make a name for ourselves and not be scattered over the face of the whole earth.'" (Genesis 11:4.)

The response of God to this plan has been interpreted as one of dismay at the notion that the people considered "joining" Him as equals. He, therefore, imposed upon them different languages so they could not understand one another, which caused them to scatter over the face of the whole earth. (Genesis 11:8, New International Version.)

After about ten generations, a man named Abram was born in Ur around 1813 BCE (Hebrew Calendar). In Genesis 12 we are informed that God told Abram to move his household to Canaan and promised to give that land to Abram's offspring. But Abram was childless. His wife, Sarai, suggested that he take her maidservant Hagar to be his wife, also. Hagar conceived; but from that point on, the relationship between Sarai and Hagar deteriorated until Hagar fled into the desert. Here Hagar was visited by an angel of the Lord who instructed her to return to her mistress Sarai and that through the birth of her son, who she should name Ishmael, there would be many descendants too numerous to count. (Genesis 16. This is an important occurrence, as we shall see in a subsequent chapter of this book.)

When Abram was ninety-nine years old, God said to him, "I am God Almighty; walk before me and be blameless." Then God confirmed His covenant with Abram saying: "No longer shall you be called Abram; your name will be Abraham, and I will make you fruitful; **I will make nations of you,** and kings will come from you. I will establish a covenant as an everlasting covenant between me and you and your descendants after you, for generations to come. I will be your God and the God of your descendants after you. The whole land of Canaan, where you are now alien, I will give as an **everlasting** possession to you and **your descendant**s after you; and I will be their God." (Genesis 17:1-8. Emphasis by author.)

Then God continued and instructed that the covenant of Abraham would be for him to undergo circumcision and that every male descendant (as well as males born to his household or bought with money from a foreigner but part of the household) should also be circumcised eight days after their birth for all generations to come as an everlasting covenant. God also stated that Abraham's wife Sarai would now be called Sarah and she would be blessed with a son, who was to be called Isaac. God continued, "As for Ishmael, I have heard you. I will surely bless him; I will make him fruitful and will greatly increase his numbers. He will be the father of twelve rulers, and I will make him into a great nation. But my covenant I will establish with Isaac, whom Sarah will bear to you by this time next year." (Genesis 17: 20-22.) Immediately, that day, Abraham, who was ninety-nine years old, and his son Ishmael, who was thirteen years old, were circumcised. After that all males in Abraham's household were circumcised. (Genesis 17:24-27.)

Sarah did bear a son who was named Isaac and when Isaac was weaned, Abraham held a celebration. After the celebration, Sarah accused Ishmael of "mocking" Isaac and demanded that Abraham get rid of the slave woman Hagar and her son Ishmael, as she feared he would claim a share of *her* son Isaac's inheritance. Abraham was distressed; but God told him to listen to Sarah. Further, God said, "I will make the son of the maidservant (Hagar) into a nation also, because he is your offspring." (Genesis 21: 8-13.)

Several generations later, Joseph, who was the grandson of Isaac and very much favored by his father Jacob, became the object of his brothers' jealousy and they sold him to traveling Ishmaelite merchants they encountered while grazing their flocks.

Joseph was taken to Egypt where he found favor with the Egyptian Pharaoh and entered into service for him. Some time later, a famine came upon the land of Canaan causing the Israelite brothers to seek help from Egypt and ultimately to reunite with Joseph, who forgave his brothers, informing them it was God's plan that he be sold to Egypt in order to save his people from the severe famine they were now experiencing. The Israelites therefore left Canaan and settled in Egypt where they remained and multiplied in number for many years.

When a new Pharaoh came to power in Egypt, he enslaved the Israelites fearing because of their increased numbers they might align themselves with Egypt's enemies and fight against him. The Israelites were thus treated harshly and their lives became bitter and difficult with manual labor either in the fields or in construction and building. During this time of harsh treatment, they continued to increase in number. At last the Pharaoh ordered all newborn boys to be thrown into the river in order to control the increase in Israelite population.

Moses and the Exodus from Egypt

One such baby boy born was saved from this threat however, when his mother placed him in a basket she had made from bul-rushes and set him afloat in the Nile River near where the Pharaoh's daughter bathed. The baby's sister, Miriam, was stationed close by to watch out for him. The Pharaoh's daughter found the baby and with the intervention of Miriam, the baby's own mother was secured to nurse him. When the child was weaned, he was returned to Pharaoh's daughter and she kept him as her own son, naming him Moses. Moses was raised as an Egyptian prince; but he eventually recognized the cruelty of the Egyptians and upon witnessing one of them beating a Hebrew, Moses became angry and killed him. Afterwards, he fled from Egypt to Midian and married. It was while tending the flock of his father-in-law, that God appeared to Moses in a burning bush and told him that he was the God of his father, the God of Abraham, Isaac and Jacob and because of the misery His people were enduring in Egypt, God directed Moses to go to the Pharaoh and request to bring the Israelites out of Egypt. When the Pharaoh refused, God sent ten plagues upon Egypt including, finally, killing the firstborn sons along with firstborn animals. God instructed the Hebrews to sacrifice a Paschal lamb (an Egyptian deity) to him and to put the lamb's blood on their doorframes. This would be a sign for the Angel of Death to spare the firstborn sons in the homes of the Israelites.

That passing over was commemorated forever by the name "Passover"–when God saved the Israelite first-born by passing over their homes while striking down the Egyptians' firstborn sons. That action finally convinced the Pharaoh to allow the exodus of the Israelites from Egypt. Without even allowing their bread to rise, the bread was baked unleavened for the Israelites' hurried departure. This unleavened bread known today as "matzo" became an integral part of the commemoration of the Passover.

Even though the Pharaoh had agreed to release the Israelites, later he regretted the decision and pursued them with an army of men and chariots to where they were camped beside the Red Sea. As the Egyptians approached, God told Moses to stretch out his hand to the sea, and "...the Lord opened up a path through the sea, with walls of water on each side; and a strong wind blew all that night, drying the sea bottom. So the people of Israel walked through the sea on dry ground."(Exodus 14: 19-22.) With the Egyptians in pursuit, and the Israelites now saved, the waters flowed over the Egyptian army and all its chariots and horsemen were drowned. God had saved the Israelites and they, at last, believed and put their trust in God and Moses, his servant.

Gods Commandments for the Israelites

For several months, the Israelites wandered from place to place in the desert, finally coming to the Desert of Sinai where they camped in front of a mountain. Initially, only Moses was permitted to approach God face to face on Mount Sinai, but God also revealed himself to the Israelites. It was on Mt. Sinai that God gave Moses the Ten Commandments, speaking these words: (Exodus 20: 2-17.)

"I am the Lord your God, who brought you out of Egypt, out of the land of slavery."

1. You shall have no other gods besides me.

2. You shall not make for yourself an idol in the form of any-thing in heaven above or on the earth beneath or in the waters below. You shall not bow down to them or worship them, for I, the Lord your God, am a jealous God, punish-ing the children for the sin of the fathers to the third and fourth generation of those who hate me, but showing love to thousands who love me and keep my commandments." (Note: This second commandment is the source of conflict among the three Abrahamic religions in that Jews, as well as Muslims, consider any likeness of human or animals as

a graven image and idol whereas Christians look at such images as visual reminders, but not idols and certainly not to be worshipped.)

3. "You shall not misuse the name of the Lord your God, for the Lord will not hold anyone guiltless who misuses his name.

4. Remember the Sabbath day by keeping it holy. "Six days you shall labor and do all your work, but the seventh day is a Sabbath to the Lord your God. On it you shall not do any work, neither you, nor your son or daughter, nor your manservant or maidservant, nor your animals, nor the alien within your gates. For in six days the Lord made the heavens and the earth, the sea, and all that is in them, but he rested on the seventh day. Therefore, the Lord blessed the Sabbath day and made it holy.

5. Honor your father and your mother, so that you may live long in the land the Lord your God is giving you.

6. You shall not murder.

7. You shall not commit adultery.

8. You shall not steal.

9. You shall not give false testimony against your neighbor.

10. You shall not covet your neighbor's house. You shall not covet your neighbor's wife, or his manservant or maidservant, his ox or donkey, or anything that belongs to your neighbor."

Until Moses's death and before the people actually entered the Promised Land, the Israelites waxed and waned in their obedience to God. The first five books of the Hebrew Bible/Old Testament—The

Torah or the Pentateuch (Genesis, Exodus, Leviticus, Numbers and Deuteronomy)—record the events from the creation to the death of Moses. However, the Torah was not written down until the 6th century BCE. There were only oral transmissions of the events that took place from one generation to the next.

In the Torah, God laid out his covenant with his people, the Israelites, and gave them 613 detailed and specific commandments (mitzvot) to follow and to live by. They were God's treasured people who were chosen for a spiritual mission in the world. Included in those commandments were dietary restrictions, clothing requirements, how to conduct daily life, both personally as well as in business and in matters of agriculture. Laws of morality were addressed including how damages should be repaid when laws were violated. The oral Torah explained how the Sabbath (Shabbat) should be kept and important festivals and celebrations were also described.

In addition to the commandments, direction was also given in the Torah on how to build and maintain a moveable sacred place to worship God—a place in which God was to "reside" (The Ark of the Covenant)—when the Israelites moved from place to place during their sojourn of many years in the desert before reaching the Promised Land.

God described precisely how worship was to be carried out as well as who could approach the Ark and lead the worship. The Torah's oral interpretations known as the Oral Law, which were given only to Moses who, in turn, taught the laws to the people. The Oral Law detailed how to carry out *all* of God's commandments and became known as the Mishnah Torah. In the event the Mosaic laws were not clear, pre-Christian rabbinic scholars and sages debated and attempted to reach consensus on the exact meanings, adding oral amplifications to the commandments. Additionally, they added their own rabbinic commandments for the purpose of preventing any accidental violation of any of the 613 God-given mitzvot and to provide further clarification of the laws.

Oral Laws Written

Around 200 CE, because of a decline and/or a scattering of teaching rabbis to many different geographic locations, Rabbi Judah, one of many, decided to record in writing, the Oral Laws in sixty-three tractates that codified the law according to topics i.e. laws for the Sabbath (Shabbat), laws for clothing, eating, business dealings etc. Because the Oral Law and its discourse were recorded by others also, often they varied according to their given schools of Jewish thought. When valid, but differing opinions occurred, the written Mishnah opinions were recorded at the side margins in the Mishnah Torah where they could be read and considered.

This became known as the Talmud. However, the Talmud itself, over time, developed variations as a result of editing—the most long-standing are the Jerusalem Talmud and the Babylonian Talmud. Of note, the Torah Scroll from which the sacred Torah is read during worship contains *only* those words given by God directly to Moses.

The rabbinic additions in the Mishnah were not new or invented mitzvot but rather clarifications of existing ones and they are considered as binding as the commandments of the Torah. Should a dispute arise however, the Torah commandments would take precedence.

There were many rabbinic scholars and sages who argued and gave opinions on the meanings of the Mishnah and the practice of mitzvot in the Talmud. Several of the most renown are Hillel the Elder (110 BCE-10 CE Babylon Talmud), Akiva be Joseph (40-137 CE Jerusalem Talmud) and Rabbi Moshe ben Maimon (1135-1204 CE Spain) also known as Maimonides.

They were major contributors of ethical principles, teachings and maxims including fundamental principles for daily conduct such as respect for yourself and others, fairness in all things, humility, kindness toward others and peaceful coexistence.

"Love your neighbor as yourself (Leviticus 19:18.) is the great principle of the Torah from which Hillel coined a version of the Golden Rule: "That which is hateful to you, do not do to your fellow man". He added, "This is the whole of the Torah; the rest is the explanation; go and learn."

Maimonides was a pious Jewish philosopher/physician who lived in the twelfth century, first in Muslim Morocco and then in Egypt. Over a period of ten years he codified Jewish law from the Mishnah Torah (by subject) into fourteen volumes called Maimonides Magnum Opus: *The Laws Concerning Character Traits** (the Book of Knowledge, the first of the fourteen books). It included eleven commandments of which five are positive: 1) to imitate God's ways, 2) to associate with those who know God, 3) to love one's neighbor/fellow Jew, 4) to love converts, and 5) to rebuke those who stray from the law.

---

* The term "character traits" is the closest English translation from the Hebrew "Laws of De'ot". These commandments clearly had a goal of tolerance, respect and loving kindness for one's brother and neighbor regardless of whether or not they were Jewish.

The six negative commandments were: 1) not to hate brothers (non-Jews or those following the Noah covenant), 2) not to put anyone to public shame, 3) not to afflict the distressed, 4) not be a talebearer, 5) not to take revenge, and 6) not to bear a grudge.

One of Maimonides' conclusions in *The Laws Concerning Character Traits* was that an individual's traits should not be at either extreme of a continuum, but rather at the mean, so to speak.

For example, one should not be overly stingy or overly extravagant and if one were at either of these extremes, then over-compensating toward the opposite extreme should correct one's actions and bring the behavior closer to the mean. This can be accomplished with practice. Thus, if one were exceedingly miserly, the antidote to bring this trait toward the "mean" of preferred behavior would be to practice being overly generous by giving much to charity. Likewise, a person should not be too "clownish" or too sad but have an appropriate temperate demeanor. When all character traits are at the "mean" this is the way of a wise man.

The importance for the perfection of character traits is for the settlement of a man's mind and when this extends to others and to the community, ultimately the world will become "stabilized". For the individual, this striving for balance of body and soul perfects and calms our health (both physically and mentally) and enables us to achieve our earthly goal, which is to find and worship God. This is the individual's highest task and explains the saying of Hillel The Elder, who as a sage and scholar, is credited with much of the interpretation of the Mishnah or Oral Laws as they are found in the Torah.

"If I am not for myself, who will be for me?"

Clearly this is not a selfish desire to live and acquire objects or power for one's self, but rather to understand that human beings should take responsibility as individuals to achieve the virtues that will enable their soul to reach its goal of finding God. It follows then, that when we neglect to improve ourselves, we are separated from that goal.

Mankind has been given the intellect and capacity to develop and achieve virtuous or wicked actions—ideal or imperfect character traits. God compels nothing; but He commands, instructs and may even render precaution, rewards and punishments. In "knowing" God and following his ways, we will not have the knowledge of God, but rather his blessings.

The Torah and the Talmud, the written and oral traditions, appear to be the deciding factor between the Reform movement of Judaism and the Orthodox movement. The Talmud is, for the Orthodox Jew, a central component, whereas today's Reform Jew rejects the Talmud's divine authority and thinks of it rather as a guide. They consider only the Hebrew Bible as a whole—the Tanakh (the complete Old Testament) the real authority.

The Jewish Tanakh

The Tanakh itself has three components: the Torah (the first five books—Genesis thru Deuteronomy orally given directly by God to Moses), the Nevi'm (the Prophets—consisting of two subgroups, the first of which are denoted as former prophets i.e. the books of Joshua,

Judges, Samuel, Kings, Isaiah, Jeremiah and Ezekiel. The second grouping is of "minor" prophets i.e. Hosea, Joel, Amos, Obadiah, Jonah, Micah, Nahum, Habakkuk, Zephaniah, Haggai, Zechariah, and Malachi.) These prophecies deal with the time period when the Israelites entered into Israel and established a permanent destination for worship and a final place for the Ark of the Covenant—the Holy of Holies. King Solomon, directed by God, built his temple as a place of worship at the site of a stone altar—the Temple Mount—where God had once directed Abraham to sacrifice Isaac. The Temple remained until the Babylonian captivity when it was destroyed. The prophecies also predicted and described the ultimate cleansing and redemption of the world with the coming of the Messiah, "the anointed one," who God promised would arrive in the future to deliver and save the Jews and to make the world a Godly abode. Through the Messiah, **all** peoples in the world would be saved.

The third portion of the Tanakh is the Ketuvim, often referred to as "writings". These, too, have several subgroupings and may contain additional prophecies. The first group is known as the poetic books (Psalms, Proverbs and Job.) The second is made up of the scrolls, five relatively short books (Song of Songs, Book of Ruth, Lamentations, Ecclesiastes and Esther) and finally, the books of Daniel, Ezra, Nehemiah and Chronicles.

Among the 613 commandments (mitzvot), which include the Ten Commandments given to Moses, it is noteworthy that those commandments dealing with relationships with others commonly say or suggest we are all neighbors. In fact, within the Ten Commandments, most important are those describing reverence to God, but also how one should live in relation to others i.e. not to steal, or murder, give false witness (lie), commit adultery, or covet thy neighbors' property. Likewise, within the mitzvot that deal with relationships, "thy neighbor" is used for both one's "fellow Jew" and others within and outside the Jewish community. Specifically, in Leviticus 19:18, it says: "Love your neighbor as yourself." Similarly, there are several other references within the Torah, for example in Exodus 22:21 and 23:9: "Do not mistreat an alien or oppress him, for you were aliens in Egypt" and in Leviticus 19:33: "When an alien lives with you in your land, do not mistreat him. The alien living with you must be treated as one of your native-born. Love him as yourself for you were aliens in Egypt."

Dispersion of Jews

The permanent temple for Jews to worship in and to house the Ark of the Covenant was built initially, as mentioned earlier, by King Solomon, a man of peace (970-931 BCE) in Jerusalem on a stone altar referred to as The Temple Mount. As a result of war and siege by the Babylonian King Nebuchadnezzar in 587 BCE, the temple was destroyed. It was rebuilt in 516 BCE, but many of the original objects, including the Ark of the Covenant, were missing and remain missing today*.

The second temple was destroyed during the Roman Empire occupation of Jerusalem in 70 CE. Thereafter, the Jews dispersed far and wide throughout the Mediterranean Basin, in northern Africa, Spain, and Europe and eventually to central Asia and Eastern Europe.

---

*   Ethiopia claims it rescued the Ark and has it protected in the church, Our Lady of Zion, in Aksum.

Curiously, the month and day of both temple destructions, as well as the expulsion from Spain of Jews who would not convert to Catholicism during the Inquisition by the Roman Catholic Church in 1492 was the 9th of Av (July) on the Jewish calendar.

With the scattering of Jews to many different locations throughout the world, the Jewish theology, although intact by way of the Torah as well as the traditions, was influenced by the many cultures of the locations they came to occupy.

The once concentrated clan of learned rabbinical scholars was no longer readily available, however, the uneducated peasantry that flourished away from intellectual centers maintained a simple, but sincere understanding of the practices of the Jewish theology. Yiddish, a Hebrew/Germanic language that came about at this time was spoken only by Jewry and was successful in binding together those of Jewish ancestry in any given region.

Mystical Kabbalah became popular, particularly in Eastern Europe, and offered esoteric interpretations of the Torah that explored the Jewish soul's progression rather than focusing on God's commandments and His covenant with the Jewish people. Traveling "teachers" who frequently visited the Jewish regions focused on developing a fervent love for God along with prayer and faith rather than scholarly interpretations of study. These teachers were often charismatic and demonstrated spiritual powers and knowledge as well as the ability to prophesize and perform miracles and healings.

In many regions these new ideas, thoughts and movements took hold and replaced the previous threats of punishment for disobedience of the traditional Jewish practices. Humble and sincere reverence to God in all of daily conduct became the focus of practice.

Origin of Hasidism and Chabad

During the 17th century, a charismatic public teacher, Israel ben Eliezer, who became known as Baal Shem Tov (Master of the Good Name) had great appeal not only with Jews, including rabbinical scholars, but non-Jewish peasants and even many Polish nobles. Baal Shem Tov was renowned for his love of every Jew and he emphasized sincerity and simplicity in his approach to Jewish practices for the uneducated.

He provided a spiritual revival for the unlearned as well as an ability to give a depth of learning for the scholarly. His Kabbalistic knowledge and practices enabled him not only to perform miracles and healings, but by telling stories and parables, he was able to meet the spiritual needs of the common folk by providing interpretations they could understand. At the same time, he was able to provide depth of learning for scholars.

He taught that a sincere love of God combined with faith and prayer from the heart, or whatever the individual was capable of, was a greater accomplishment in the eyes of God than a fully observant Jew who lacked zeal and inspiration. The disciples and followers of Baal Shem Tov set his teachings in writing and the movement, Hasidism, was born. It initially centered in Ukraine but quickly spread throughout Eastern Europe in the 1800's. Its concept was that of a mentor and guide as well as a mediator or "righteous one"–a Tzadik or saint referred to as "Rebbe"—through whom God sent earthly blessings concerning health and life, livelihood and children.

The Tzadik or Rebbe was a man who was often supported by the community so that he might be in deep contemplation with God. Although following the traditional, law-oriented Judaism remained important, Hasidic Judaism encompassed spirituality through Jewish mysticism with saintly leaders who were intercessors with the Divine on behalf of followers.

Hasidism, although there are many versions, shares an emphasis on the sincerity of deeds and prayer by *all* people, be they common folk or scholars. Devotion, good deeds and serving God with joyfulness are viewed as a spiritual equality with that of the scholarly, who were expected to have a greater depth of learning and understanding. Hasidic philosophy teaches a Divine presence in everything and everyone.

Chabad spirituality is one of the Hasidic variances and was founded by Schneur Zalman of Liadi (1745-1813). This Hasidic branch sees the continual intellectual development of one's mind at every level of education as an important aspect of Judaism and includes as a priority, the dissemination of Hasidic philosophy to all Jews. Devotion and piety were not just concerned with "do's and don'ts" but rather that every person connects to God at their own level.

Return to Israel

After the Holocaust most survivors either moved to Israel or America (New York and New Jersey) and many Hasidic communities were established in the U. S.. Today, Hasidic Jewry is considered the most orthodox branch of Judaism and those who practice this version adhere to specifically defined prayers, worship, dress, daily ritual, social requirements and restrictions. Of the 14.2 million Jews in the world today one million, or 7.0% of the population, are Hasidic.

The Jewish Bible (the Tanakh), as noted previously, ends after the Ketuvim. Throughout the prophecies, the writings and Psalms of the Jewish Tanakh, there are many references regarding the coming of the Messiah to save the world from the conflict that separates not only man from man, but also man from God. The Messiah (Moshiach) will free the Jewish people from all nations and they will return to Israel where the Holy Temple in Jerusalem will be rebuilt. The topic of the Messiah is a clear and strong separation of beliefs between Jewish and "other" religious doctrines.

Whereas Jesus is acknowledged as the Messiah in the Christian theology, for Jews and Muslims, Jesus was a prophet. Accordingly, in Jewish thought, the One God cannot have a Son nor a Holy Spirit, as that would not fit the definition of a monotheistic God and God commands that there be only *one* God. Despite several reputed Jews who claimed to have been the "messiah" (they were eventually disproven), the Jews continue to await the Messiah who is yet to come. They believe that the prophets Jesus and Muhammad have provided the groundwork for the coming Moshiach/Messiah who, when he arrives, will unite all nations with a single religion that will bind all peoples together to create peace. The universal goal will then be to seek and attain understanding and knowledge of God—a goal that eliminates the desire for people to harm one another. Through the Jewish people, it is believed; *all* people will therefore be saved.

MAJOR JEWISH HOLIDAYS

Shabbat

The origin of Shabbat or "the Sabbath" is thought to be after the six days of creation. "By the seventh day, God had finished the work he had been doing; and so, on the seventh day, he rested from all his work. And God blessed the seventh day and made it holy. "(Genesis 2:2-3.) Observing the seventh day of the week as a holy day was also the 5th of the Ten Commandments. Resting does not however mean sleeping late but rather it is a cessation of work and the daily routine in order to re-create the spirit and restore the soul. The Sabbath begins at sundown on Friday evening and ends twenty-five hours later on Saturday evening. Candles are lit, prayers are offered, and God is praised (rather than receiving requests since God is resting too).

A portion of the Torah is read either on Friday night or Saturday morning or both. The Torah scrolls are brought forth out of the Ark as the congregation rises for the preparation. The same readings from the Torah are read around the world for each Shabbat. Singing may take place by a cantor or vocalist.

The Sabbath should be sanctified, and this is accomplished at the Kiddush after candles are lit, prayers recited, and the Torah is read. Wine and challah bread may be used to symbolize the joy of life in Judaism, but a blessing over Shabbat itself—the day of rest—is also important. The Kiddush sanctification is recited:

> "Blessed art Thou, O Lord our God, King of the universe, who hath hallowed us by Thy commandments and hast taken pleasure in us, and in love and favor hast given us Thy holy Sabbath as an inheritance, a memorial of the creation—that day being also the first day of the holy convocations, in remembrance of the departure from Egypt. For Thou hast chosen us and hallowed us above all nations, and in love and favor hast given us Thy holy Sabbath as an inheritance. Blessed art Thou, O Lord, who hallowest the Sabbath."

To conclude Shabbat on Saturday evening, the Havdalah service is held so that one may be introduced back into one's routine once again. A braided candle or a candle with more than one wick is lit and again wine may be used to symbolize the joy of life in Judaism. Sweet spices are smelled as one's five senses again become engaged with routine daily living. The following is recited:

> "Blessed art thou, God, our Lord, King of the Universe
> Who distinguishes
> Holiness from the everyday,
> Light from dark,
> Israel from the nations,
> The seventh day from the six workdays.
> Blessed art thou, God,
> Who distinguishes holiness from the everyday."

Rosh Hashanah

Rosh Hashanah is the beginning of a new year. It is a time of judgment and a time in which hearts and lives can be revised in order to live a life more attuned to God's commandments. Rosh Hashanah is the beginning of a ten-day period of self-examination, repentance and prayer and it is observed on the first day of the Hebrew month of Tishrei, which coincides with September or October on the secular calendar. It is a deeply religious occasion and is ritually prepared for a month prior to the actual days. Although Reform congregations may only celebrate one day, Conservative and Orthodox Jews observe two days. The shofar, made from a ram's horn, is sounded during the month before Rosh Hashanah; it is a wakeup call from complacency, so that believers might be moved to reflect and repent.

The shofar itself is used to represent God's testing of Abraham when he was commanded to sacrifice his son Isaac. When Abraham showed his readiness to follow God's command, the Lord provided a ram to be sacrificed instead.

The shofar may be blown with four different sounds, suggesting different accountings of the activities of the past year. Prayers in both the synagogue and at home emphasize God's judgment as well as a plea for God's forgiveness.

A symbolic ceremony called Tashlich is also a tradition at Rosh Hashanah and may take place near a body of water so that one may cast their sins and wrongdoings into the water using breadcrumbs to represent their iniquities. Psalms or verses from Micah 7: 18-19 are recited:

"Who is a God like you, who pardons sin and forgives the transgression of the remnant of his inheritance? You do not stay angry forever but delight to show mercy. You will tread our sins underfoot and hurl all our iniquities into the depths of the seas."

A family dinner with blessings of wine and bread is a tradition for this holiday. The bread for this occasion is called challah and is round and/or braided rather than oblong. Apples dipped in honey are eaten in hopes of a "sweet" year to come. Wishes for a good year are in the form of the greeting "L'shanah tovah!"

Yom Kippur

This day occurs ten days after Rosh Hashanah and is part of the High Holidays—Yom Kippur being the holiest. The interim days between Rosh Hashanah and Yom Kippur are to be spent in reflection on the previous year in regard to one's behavior and misdeeds. The literal translation of Yom Kippur is "Day of Atonement" and is the time for rededication of mind, body and soul to forgive and be forgiven by one's acquaintances as well as to be reconciled with God and self. The Sabbath (Shabbat) between Rosh Hashanah and Yom Kippur is known as "the Sabbath of Return"—"return, O Israel!"

On this day, the commandment is to go to those who were wronged, acknowledging one's sin and the pain it may have caused them, and seek their forgiveness. Likewise, one must also be willing to forgive others and dismiss any feeling of resentment *their* wrongdoings might have caused. One both seeks and gives pardon and afterward can then turn to God to seek forgiveness and atonement. It is an act of self-purification and an opportunity to remove the effects of misdeeds by self-denial in the form of fasting, a sign that one is able to rise above the most basic biological needs to give attention to matters of the spirit. From the age of twelve for girls and thirteen for boys (unless there is a medical condition) a twenty-four-hour fast without food or drink is required. During this time, fasting, praying, studying, reflecting and concentrating on the biblical texts all contribute to the full meaning of the Yom Kippur experience.

It is one of the 613 commandments to attend worship on Yom Kippur when the Torah is read along with a memorial service to remember loved ones who have died. A special chant, solely for Yom Kippur, annuls any unintended actions made during the previous year and one is expected to reflect on how to lead meaningful lives in the coming year by eliminating the previous missteps during the year that has just ended.

Yom Kippur is a new beginning. It is atonement for transgressions against others and most importantly against God. Families should be at peace with one another and it follows also to perpetuate the memory of loved ones by visiting the cemetery the day before Yom Kippur or giving to a charity as a gesture of concern for others in need. After the twenty-four-hour fast, the shofar is again sounded and a joyous "break-the-fast" meal is eaten either with the congregation or at home.

Pesach (Passover)

Passover begins on the 15th day of the month of Nissan, which coincides with a time in the month of April. The holiday continues for eight days and it's again a commandment to observe it.

"This is a day you are to commemorate; for the generations to come you shall celebrate it as a festival to the Lord—a lasting ordinance. For seven days you are to eat bread made without yeast. On the first day remove the yeast from your houses, for whoever eats anything with yeast in it from the first day through the seventh must be cut off from Israel. On the first day hold a sacred assembly, and another one on the seventh day. Do no work at all on these days, except to prepare food for everyone to eat—that is all you may do. Celebrate the Feast of Unleavened Bread, because it was on this very day that I brought your division out of Egypt. Celebrate this day as a lasting ordinance for the generations to come." (Exodus 12:14-17.)

This holiday commemorates God leading the Israelites out of Egypt where the Egyptians enslaved them for many years. The "Passover" refers to the last of the plagues sent by God to the Pharaoh to convince him to release the Jews from bondage after the Pharaoh refused Moses' pleas to let them go. This plague involved the slaying of the firstborn sons in Egypt by God.

In order to save the firstborn sons of the Israelites, God instructed the Hebrews to sacrifice a lamb and to put the blood from the sacrifice on the sides and top of the doorframe as a sign that the house was that of an Israelite and should be passed over by the Angel of Death. God further instructed them to commemorate forever this "passing over".

As this came to pass and the Egyptian firstborn sons were slain, including the Pharaoh's firstborn son, the Pharaoh ordered the Israelites to leave as quickly as they could. Without enough time to allow their bread to rise, the Israelites prepared to leave Egypt. As part of the Passover remembrance, only unleavened bread is eaten for the duration of the commemoration and there should be no food containing yeast in the house. The entire house is thoroughly cleaned and grain flour and items used to make bread are disposed of and purchased anew after the holiday. Matzah (matzo) is eaten during this period of eight days when the prohibited yeast bread is not available. On the day before Pesach, the firstborn son should fast to remember the Passover from the Egyptian slayings. There should be no work on the first two days and the last two days of Pesach.

On the first night of Pesach, a special meal called a Seder is full of meaning and reminders of the Passover event. The word Seder means "order" as the sequence or order of events during this dinner is important. It's a festive event that celebrates the Israelites transition from slavery to freedom. A special book, The Haggadah, guides and explains the meaning of each part of the Seder.

At every Seder there is a special Seder plate, which is divided into six sections with six symbolic foods on it. The traditional contents are: A hard-boiled egg—a symbol of spring (when Passover takes place) but also the tenacity of the Jewish people as "the more the egg is boiled, the harder is becomes"; lettuce as a bitter herb; a lamb shank bone to represent the Paschal lamb that was sacrificed and the blood used to mark the doors of the Israelites so the Angel of Death would know to "pass over" their houses and not kill the first-born sons of those households; a mixture of apple, nuts and spices mixed together to represent the mortar the Hebrew slaves used to build Egyptian structures; parsley dipped into salt water to remember the tears of the Jewish slaves in Egypt; and bitter herbs (usually horseradish) to symbolize the bitterness of the Egyptian slavery.

The two bitter herbs are present to fulfill the commandment to eat the paschal lamb "with unleavened bread and bitter herbs (plural)". There are also three matzos stacked and wrapped together. The outer two matzos represent the double amount of manna God provided for the Jews when they were in the dessert. The inner matzo will be used for the Seder. There may also be a cup of wine for the prophet Elijah who is said to visit every Jewish home on Passover. Elijah prophesized the coming of the Messiah one day and the age of peace and freedom the Messiah's presence on earth will bring for *all* peoples.

The order of the Seder service is as follows:

1. The Kiddush blessing proclaiming the holiness of the holiday is recited. Candles are lit and the first of four cups of wine are drunk. Eating of matzo and drinking the wine are accomplished by leaning to the left to represent reclining. Only "free" people could recline while eating and drinking during the time of the exodus.

2. Hands are washed in a prescribed manner.

3. A vegetable dipped into saltwater is eaten to represent spring and freedom—the saltwater a reminder of the tears of the Jewish slaves in Egypt.

4. The middle matzo of the three wrapped together is broken in two to remember the parting of the Red Sea. One part is put aside for later and the smaller portion placed back between the other two whole matzos.

5. Next is the telling of the story of the exodus from Egypt. It is during this time that the four questions are asked traditionally by a child. "Why is this night different from all other nights?" "Why only matzo?" "Why the dipping of bitter herbs and reclining like kings?" These questions trigger the highlight of the Seder ceremony—the retelling of the story of the Jews exodus from Egypt complete with a description of the suffering imposed upon the Israelites, the plagues upon the Egyptians and the miracles that occurred as the Jews were released from their bondage.

6. The second washing of hands with a blessing before eating more food.

7. Eating from the top and middle matzo (at least one ounce) remembering the departure from Egypt that was so rapid, the bread had not risen.

8. Eating of the bitter herbs (horseradish) to taste the bitterness of slavery.

9. Eating a sandwich of the matzo and bitter herb to fulfill the commandment of Numbers 9:11 (told to Moses) *"They are to celebrate it on the fourteenth day of the second month at twilight.*

They are to eat the lamb, together with unleavened bread and bitter herbs."

10. Eating the full Seder dinner that traditionally includes a hard-boiled egg, matzo ball soup, gefilte fish, meat and vegetables.

11. After the meal, the half-matzo broken earlier and hidden, is found and eaten as dessert as the matzo of freedom. This concludes the dinner.

12. The third cup of wine and the after-meal blessing is recited while again "reclining" or leaning to the left. At this time the door is opened for Elijah to enter as the invitation to the prophet is recited.

13. Songs of Praise to the Almighty for his unique and special guidance and care of the Jewish people. A fourth cup of wine is blessed and drunk reclining.

14. Finally a prayer that God accept this service to him and the remembrance of his saving his people by their deliverance from Egypt to the Promised Land. The service is ended with the phrase "Next year in Jerusalem" in hopes that all Jews will reunite in peaceful Jerusalem in a world of peace and freedom.

Sukkot — Feast of Booths

This is a celebration founded by a commandment from God as described in Leviticus 23:40-43. It occurred initially after a gathering of crops and lasts for seven days in thanksgiving for the bountiful agricultural blessings from God.

> "On the first day you are to take choice fruit from the trees, and palm fronds, leafy branches and poplars, and rejoice before the Lord your God for seven days. Celebrate this as a festival to the Lord for seven days each year. This is to be a lasting ordinance for generations to come—celebrate it in the seventh month. Live in booths for seven days: all native-born Israelites are to live in booths so your descendants will know that I had the Israelites live in booths when I brought them out of Egypt. I am the Lord your God."

The booths, or *sukkots*, are constructed for this festival and typically have three sides, one of which can be an existing wall such as the side of another structure. The roof is usually covered with loose branches. The celebration is one of thankful rejoicing and the sukkots are used for extending hospitality—entertaining and partaking of meals together with family and friends. Symbols of the harvest in the form of date palm fronds, willow and myrtle branches, and citron are bound together and waved in six directions—north, south, east, west, up and down to acknowledge that God is found in all directions and is omnipresent. Special prayers are recited to commemorate this occasion.

Hanukkah or Festival of the Lights

This holiday does not have its origin from the Jewish Bible; it is from a historical event that was recorded in a collection of writings known as the Apocrypha, which are of unknown authorship and origin. The holiday is based on the remembrance of a Syrian tyrant who sent his soldiers into Jerusalem to desecrate the Temple in 168 BCE. Judaism was abolished and the Jewish altar was replaced with idols and the worship of Greek gods. The Jews were either to convert to that religion or be killed.

A resistance movement was led by Judah Maccabee, but its supporters were severely outnumbered and faced overwhelming odds. Despite the odds, the Jews decisively overcame the Syrians and preserved the Jewish autonomy from assimilation into the Hellenistic culture. Upon reentering the Temple to rededicate and purify it after the Syrian defilement with Greek idols, the eternal light, which was to burn continually in the Temple, was relit. There was, however, only a single jar of oil available—only one day's supply. A messenger, sent to secure more oil, took eight days to return; but miraculously the light continued to burn the entire eight days. The rabbis of the Talmud denoted this as the Miracle of the Single Jar of Oil.

Hanukkah has, despite its radical difference in origin, become associated with Christmas and many Jewish families practice gift giving. It has, however, no association with Christmas, but rather it is a holiday celebrating family and reinforcing Jewish identity in events with seeming insurmountable odds. It is celebrated beginning on the 25th day of the Hebrew month of Kislev (corresponding to December) and it lasts for eight days. The Talmud instructs that each person in a household recites blessings while candles are lit. Candles are lit each night beginning with the far-right side of the eight-branched menorah. As additional candles are added to the left of the original one, the candles are relit each night beginning with the newest and then those to the right.

Although Hanukkah is a home-based celebration, it should also be a public proclamation of the miraculous events that occurred when the Temple was reclaimed, and the eternal light was relit and remained lit for eight days with only a small amount of oil. The Hanukkah candles are lit at sundown and if possible, a menorah is placed in a window or where it can be seen from the outside. Many cities and towns hold public menorah-lighting ceremonies.

Other things associated with Hanukkah include Torah readings taken from the book of Numbers that recount the dedication of the moveable place of worship by the Israelites in the desert. Foods cooked in oil, such as potato latkes and doughnuts are eaten in remembrance of the small amount of oil that burned for eight days.

Children play a game of chance using a dreidel or "spinning top" in which they put chocolate "coins" in a center "pot". The dreidel has a Hebrew letter on each of its four sides—nun (take nothing from the pot), gimmel (take everything from the pot), hey (take half of the pot), and shin (put one coin in the pot). When the dreidel is spun, the letter obtained guides the taking or putting coins into the pot. The Hebrew letters also form an acronym NGHS: "Neis gadol hayah sham" which means, "A great miracle happened there".

Purim

This festival occurs on the 14th of the Hebrew month of Adar—late winter/early spring. It celebrates, again, the tenacity of the Jewish people in surviving a plot to destroy and annihilate them. As this story goes, the Persian Empire during the 4th century BCE extended over 127 lands, which included all Jews as subjects. The Persian king, having executed his wife for failing to follow his orders, sought to find a new queen by holding a beauty contest. A Jewish girl, Esther, became the new queen even though her identity and nationality were unknown.

When Haman was appointed by the king as prime minister, Esther's cousin Mordechai refused to bow to him as was required by the king's orders. Haman, who hated Jews, persuaded the king to issue a decree to exterminate all the Jews on the 13th of Adar. Mordechai convinced the Jews to repent, fast and pray to God. Esther then invited both the king and Haman to a feast and during the feast revealed her identity as being Jewish. The king ordered Haman to be hanged and for Mordechai to replace him as prime minister. The Jews were granted the right to worship as they pleased and to defend themselves against their enemies.

To commemorate this event, the book of Esther is read to recount the miracle, money is given to the poor, and gifts of food are given to friends. There is often a feast with special, filled cookies called "Hamantaschen" (Haman's pockets) made and eaten. Costume parties are a customary manner of celebration for this event.

Summary and Additional Comments

No other group of people in world history can proclaim to have had a personal relationship with God such as that of the Jews. At their origin, God singled out a simple man, Abraham, for perhaps no other reason than he was a good man in a world with a population that had, for the most part, forgotten the seven Noahic commandments given generations before to Noah by God. It contained His covenant never again to destroy the earth by flood.

God could not give up on the world with a people that were created in His own image and assessed by God as *"very good"*. (Genesis 1:31.) Perhaps another plan was in order. God's promise to Abraham was that of a binding love and a declaration that he and his descendants were to be a chosen people—chosen not as a favorite; but rather, chosen with a responsibility. Abraham was required to be faithful to the one God and follow His commandments, which began with God's direction for him to go to a new land and found a new people through his descendants. It is unknown if Abraham saw Yahweh (Hebrew name for God), but it is said that he heard his voice.

Eventually, due to a famine, the Israelites ended up in Egypt where after many years, an unkind and insecure Pharaoh forced them into hard labor. By God's intervention and against enormous odds, the people chosen by God were led to freedom with Moses as their leader. To Moses, God revealed himself personally and visually on Mount Sinai and indirectly, with visual evidence of God, to the Israelites waiting for Moses to come down from the mountain from his encounter and meeting with Yahweh.

This small group of people who have always been a minority in number was and perhaps will be yet, the instrument of God's will. They have endured for centuries—a miracle in itself—and God has repeatedly intervened to save them from annihilation, first in Egypt, then from the Babylonians, the Romans, the Persians, the Holocaust and even currently with Iran.

Always the underdog and often scorned, they were forced to scatter to the ends of the earth after the Roman siege of Jerusalem. Yet they have always remembered who they were even though they were, at times, segregated by law to live apart and to be treated as pariahs.

Not until after the French Revolution, as a by-product of the French victory in human rights, did Europe recognize them to have these rights also. But the newly acquired rights barely lasted a century before Hitler attempted to eradicate the Jews with a plot so horrific that it's nearly impossible to imagine how a civilized society could acquiesce to such a scheme.

To the Jews, it seems that God continues to intervene in human history for them to survive, even if it often appears to be at the last possible moment. Many argue, how could a *loving* God allow an event such as the Holocaust to occur? Yet, for the Jews who continue to be faithful, this is not their concern. With the miracle of their historical land returned to them after World War II to once again provide them with a nation of their own, they wait and persevere in their faith, for whatever the role God has for them in the evolution of mankind.

Whether orthodox in practice or liberal in interpretation of these practices, every Jew is family and they take pride to be a part of that family and wait to serve whatever purpose God has for them. As of this writing, it is currently the Hebrew year 5778.

References/Bibliography

Holy Bible: New International Version.

Armstrong, K. (1997). *Jerusalem: One city, three faiths*. New York: Ballantine Books.

Armstrong, K. (1993). *A history of God: The 4,000-year quest of Judaism, Christianity and New York*: Ballantine Books.

Chabad.org. "What is Purim?" Retrieved March 21,2016, from http://www.chabad.org/holidays/purim.

Chabad.org. "Passover: The Seder service in a nutshell." Retrieved March 17, 2016, From http://www.chabad.org/holidays/passover/pesach.

Engelbrecht, E. A. (Ed.). (2013). *Concordia's complete Bible handbook*, Second Edition. St. Louis, Mo: Concordia Publishing.

Greenberg, B. (1985). *How to run a traditional Jewish household*. New York: Simon & Schuster.

Hersch, I. H. (1907). "The French revolution and the emancipation of the Jews." *The Jewish Quarterly*, 19(3), 540-565. Stable URL: http://www.jstor.org/stable/1450957

Jacobs, L. (1995). "My Jewish learning: Hillel." (from The Jewish religion: A companion). Retrieved January 16, 2016, from http://myjewishlearning.com/Hillel.

Jones, R. (2011). "Jewish prophecy suggests Messiah may be coming soon". Retrieved February 22, 2016, from http://www.israeltoday.co.il/News/tabid/178/nid/23021.

Judaism 101. "Pesach: Passover". Retrieved March 8, 2016, from http://www.jewfaq.org/holidaya.htm.

Judaism 101. "A list of the 613 mitzvot (commandments)". Retrieved January 21/2016, from http://www.jewfaq.org/613.htm.

Mendel, N. (1999). *Rabbi Schneur Zalman of Liadi: A biography of the first Labavitcher Rebbe*. Brooklyn, New York: Kehot Publication Society.

Reform Judaism.org. "Rosh HaShana". Retrieved March 3, 2016, from http://reformjudaism.org/jewish-holidays/rosh-hashanah.

Reform Judaism.org. "Yom Kippur". Retrieved March 3, 2016, from http://www.reformjudaism.org/jewish-holidays/yom-kippur-day- atonement.

Reform Judaism.org. "Sukkot- Feast of Booths". Retrieved March 3, 2016, from http://www.reformjudaism.org/jewish-holidays/sukkot.

Reform Judaism.org. "Hanukkah". Retrieved March 3, 2016, from http://www.reformjudaism.org/print/node/11896.

Reform Judaism.org. "Origins of Shabbat". Retrieved March 3, 2016, from http://www.reformjudaism.org/origins-shabbat.

Robinson, G. (2000). *Essential Judaism: A complete guide to beliefs, customs, and Rituals*. New York: Pocket Books (Division of Simon and Schuster).

Sacks, J. (2000). *The dignity of difference: How to avoid the clash of civilizations*. New York: Continuum.

Smith, H. (1991). *The World's Religions*. New York: HarperCollins.

Stiel, D. (from ReformJudaism.org). "What to expect at a Passover Seder"? Retrieved March 17, 2016, from http://www.reformjudaism.org/print/node/48081.

Weiss, R.L. with Butterworth, C. (Eds.). (1983). *Ethical writings of Maimonides*. New York: Dover Publications.

Wikipedia contributors. "The Talmud". In Wikipedia, The free encyclopedia, Retrieved January 13, 2016, from https://en.wikipedia.org/wiki/Talmud.

Wikipedia contributors. "Ishmael". In Wikipedia, The free encyclopedia, Retrieved January 9, 2016, from https://en.wikipedia.org/wiki/Ishamel.

Wikipedia contributors. "Hasidic Judaism". In Wikipedia, The free encyclopedia, Retrieved February 25, 2016, from https://en.wikipedia.org/wiki/Hasidic_Judaism.

Wikipedia contributors. "Moses". In Wikipedia, The free encyclopedia, Retrieved January 9, 2016, from https://en.wikipedia.org/wiki/Moses.

Wouk, H. (1987). *This is my God.* (1988). New York: Hatchett Books (Little, Brown And Company.

✝

CHRISTIANITY

Prophesies of the New Covenant

Although there are several vague references to the coming of the Messiah in the Torah itself, the most definitive references contained in the Hebrew Bible (the Old Testament) are in the prophets' portion, two of which are the prophets Isaiah and Zechariah.

Previous to these prophetic revelations however, God spoke to David through the prophet Nathan as recorded in chapter 17 of I Chronicles, verses 11-12, 14.

> "When you (David) die and are buried with your ancestors, I will make one of your sons king (this is Solomon) and will keep his kingdom strong. He will be the one to build a temple for me, and I will make sure that his dynasty continues forever.... I will put him in charge of my people and my kingdom forever. His dynasty will never end."

The prophet Isaiah devotes the whole of chapter 53 to describe the "servant of the Lord" who will succeed in the task of rescuing the people of the Lord, who continually fall into sinful ways.

"After the suffering of his soul, he will see the light of life and be satisfied; by his knowledge my righteous servant will justify many, and he will bear their iniquities." (Verse 11.)

In Isaiah Chapter 9, more words are recorded regarding what the Lord Almighty is determined to do. Verses 6-7, "A child is born to us! A son is given to us! And he will be our ruler, He will be called, Wonderful Counselor, Mighty God, Eternal Father, Prince of Peace. His royal power will continue to grow; his kingdom will always be at peace. He will rule as King David's successor, basing his power on right and justice, from now until the end of time."

In Zechariah 9:9 it is written, "Rejoice, rejoice, people of Zion! Shout for joy, you people of Jerusalem! Look, your king is coming to you! He comes triumphant and victorious, but humble and riding a donkey—on a colt, the foal of a donkey."

Even with these prophesies, the people of Zion, the chosen of the Lord, continued to disobey and sin. In Jeremiah 31: 31- 34, the Lord says, "The time is coming when I will make a new covenant with the people of Israel and with the people of Judah. It will not be like the old covenant that I made with their ancestors when I took them by the hand and led them out of Egypt. Although I was like a husband to them, they did not keep that covenant. The new covenant that I will make with the people of Israel with be this: I will put my law within them and write it on their hearts. I will be their God, and they will be my people. None of them will have to teach his fellow countryman to know the Lord, because all will know me, from the least to the greatest. I will forgive their sins and I will no longer remember their wrongs. I, the Lord, have spoken."

Here it seems that God is saying there will be no more direct contact between God and his people, but rather, an intuitive realization—a conscience, perhaps? The expectation is that people will acknowledge this innate presence of God and follow his commandments through Jesus, who is God manifested incarnate and who came physically into the world to teach mankind, by example, how their lives should be conducted with righteousness and compassion for one another and with devotion to God.

The good news regarding the new covenant is also expressed in Isaiah 56 verses 1-2: The Lord says to his people, "Do what is just and right, for soon I will save you. I will bless those who always observe the Sabbath and do not misuse it. I will bless those who do nothing evil." Further along, in verses 6-8, the Lord says to those foreigners who become part of his people, who love him and serve him, who observe the Sabbath and faithfully keep his covenant: "I will bring you to Zion, my sacred hill, give you joy in my house of prayer, and accept the sacrifices you offer on my altar. My Temple will be called a house of prayer for the people of ALL nations. The Sovereign Lord, who has brought his people home from exile to Israel, has promised that he will bring still other people to join them."

The Birth of Jesus

With this foretelling within the Hebrew Bible or the Old Testament, the New Testament begins with the birth of Jesus, the promised Savior, through whom God will fulfill the prophecies of the Old Testament. Jesus is the great Teacher who has the authority to interpret the Law of God because he IS God incarnate.

The Gospel of Matthew begins with Jesus's genealogy, which is listed by name from Abraham to Joseph, Jesus's earthly father. There are fourteen generations from Abraham to David, fourteen from David to the Jewish exile in Babylon and fourteen additional generations from then to the Messiah's birth.

Following the listing of descendants, Matthew continues with a description of the events surrounding the birth of Jesus. His mother Mary, is pregnant not by her betrothed, Joseph, who is a direct descendant of David, but miraculously by the Holy Spirit. Previously, an angel visited Joseph and informed him of God's plan and that he should wed Mary without fear or hesitation. Of the four gospels, Matthew and Luke explain the details of the events of Jesus's birth with the most description. The gospels of Mark and John begin their historical accounts of the life of Jesus beginning with John the Baptist, who baptized Jesus before he began his earthly ministry of teaching and preaching.

As previously described, the birth and life of Jesus were foretold in the Hebrew Bible/Old Testament. Even though the Hebrew people continued to disobey God's laws and to sin, over and over again God saved them in times of turmoil and war. Yet, over and over again they continued to revert to their sinful ways.

With the coming of Jesus, the Christ, people had the opportunity to witness first-hand not only how God wanted his people to live and treat one another, but, by the miracles and healings that were performed by Jesus for all to see, people would also know and forever recognize the mighty power and goodness of the Lord. Thereafter, all that would be necessary, by the new covenant, would be the acceptance of Jesus (and therefore God). When Jesus would no longer be on earth physically, the third manifestation of Almighty God, the Holy Spirit, would be sent to dwell as a guide within believers.

Typically this might take place at baptism when an individual acknowledges a desire to live a life pleasing to God without sin. One's sins are symbolically washed away so that God, in the form of the Holy Spirit, can become part of the baptized individual's soul and inner being. These actions explain the Christian Holy Trinity with God manifested in three ways: the all-powerful, beyond our capacity to fully comprehend Father God; the Son Jesus who took physical form to teach God's desires and expectations; and the Holy Spirit, which is omnipresent when invited into one's life as a guide to righteous living. All of these manifestations are, however, of the One, all-powerful, God.

Jesus was the physical example of how mankind should live and follow God's Mosaic commandments. Through the teachings of Jesus's stories and parables, humans would learn how to live with tolerance, compassion and humbleness when dealing with others.

The Life of Jesus—Baptism, Teaching and Healing

After the birth of Jesus, very little about his early years was recorded with the exception of his appearance at the temple when he was twelve years old and he acknowledged his earthly duties as promised by God, the Father. Then, nearly twenty years after this event, John the Baptist began preaching of the emergence of Jesus into public life.

John the Baptist was also the man the prophet Isaiah announced when he said: "A voice cries out, prepare in the wilderness a road for the LORD! Clear the way in the desert for our God! Fill every valley; level every mountain. The hills will become a plain, and the rough country will be smooth. Then the glory of the LORD will be revealed. And all mankind will see it. The LORD himself has promised this." (Isaiah 40: 3-5.)

The *voice* was that of John the Baptist who was an unlikely wild sort of man, but was sent by God to lay the groundwork for the ministry of Jesus on earth. John's proclamation was that "the Kingdom of heaven is near"; therefore, one should turn away from sin, be sorry for one's sins and repent for them. Using the concrete analogy of washing away one's sin by baptism in the Jordon River, John traveled throughout Judea proclaiming this message.

At the age of thirty, Jesus came to John to be baptized. Even though John declared that it was Jesus who should baptize him, Jesus persuaded him saying, "Let it be so for now. For in this way we shall do all that God requires." (Matthew 3:15). The biblical account reports that as Jesus came out of the water of the Jordon River, the heavens opened and the Holy Spirit of God came down as a dove and stayed with Jesus as a sign that henceforth He would be the one to baptize with the Holy Spirit. At that moment a voice spoke out from heaven: "This is my own dear Son, with whom I am pleased" (Matthew 3: 17, Mark 4: 11, Luke 3:22.)

God then led Jesus into the desert for forty days and nights without food. As are all humans, Satan tempted him with offers of food, power and riches in exchange for devotion to him (Satan). But Jesus rejected those notions of Satan saying, "Go away, Satan! For it is written: Worship the Lord your God and serve only him." (Matthew 4: 10, Luke 4: 8.)

After the temptations, Jesus began his earthly work and in doing so, he chose twelve Jewish disciples who traveled with him throughout his ministry and then established the Christian church after his earthly task was completed and he returned to God. Jesus lived and taught throughout Galilee in synagogues as well as where crowds gathered. Matthew 4:24-25 tells us that news of him spread throughout Syria, Decapolis, Jerusalem, Judea and from across the Jordan; and people brought to him those who were ill with disease, those who suffered pain, were demon-possessed, epileptics or paralytics.

Jesus healed them all regardless of who they were and what their status or societal position was. In addition to healing, Jesus performed many miracles such as walking on water, the feeding of a crowd with only a small amount of food and changing water into wine—to name a few. He taught whoever came to him and in his most renowned teaching, the Sermon on the Mount, he blessed those who lived their lives with love, humility, mercy, compassion and spirituality. His purpose, he assured his followers, was not to change or abolish any of God's previous laws (the Mosaic laws), but solely to teach and demonstrate how to fulfill them. He cautioned the crowds that followed him not to be as the Jewish Pharisees who made public spectacle of their worship, but to carry out the commandments privately, and with sincerity. He ministered to the rich and the poor and warned that one could not serve both God and money.

The Message of Jesus for ALL People

Jesus welcomed sinners, both Gentiles and Jews, teaching them how to live with one another, including love without judgment for one's enemies. He preached on charity and putting one's trust in God. He instructed his followers how to pray. He taught using parables and stories that by analogy relayed spiritual, moral principles with the use of living examples—often with multiple meanings and applications. His teaching of the Sermon on the Mount encapsulated the heart of God's message and his purpose on earth i.e. how to live according to God's commandments.

Jesus manifested as human to first of all save the "lost sheep" of Israel. In his parable of the shepherd who risked ninety-nine other sheep to save one that strayed, Jesus demonstrated God's absolute love for every single being. The Sanhedrin however; the official Jewish "court" of the Sadducees and Pharisees, who interpreted civil and religious Mosaic laws, looked upon his ministry with scorn even though the teachings dealt entirely with the laws of Moses.

The message of Jesus was based on love and kindness. He stressed humbleness and humility and his message was inclusive of all people. He openly chastised the Sanhedrin for being hypocrites, who espoused the laws to others but neglected it themselves, not practicing justice, mercy and forgiveness but conducting their duties for show. Jesus was a rabbi and sent his disciples to first of all visit the synagogues, but also to welcome and preach to all people, beseeching them to love and be kind to one another and to love God above all else—the giver of all of life and to whom all must answer.

Jesus preached for approximately three years; yet, even after all the miraculous signs, many who heard him were afraid they would be put out of the synagogue—fearing the Sanhedrin more than God. Finally, the time came when Jesus was prepared to carry out God's plan and to sacrifice his life in order to pay the debt for a sinful mankind. As he called his disciples for a last meal together, Jesus relayed to them the coming events of his betrayal, his denial (the way of man), his crucifixion (the payment of his life to absolve man's debt of sin) and his subsequent resurrection and victory over death.

The Crucifixion of Christ

According to John 15: 12-16, Jesus left his disciples with the following words: "This is my commandment: Love one another as I have loved you. A man can have no greater love than to lay down his life for his friends. You are my friends if you do what I command. I shall not call you servants anymore, because a servant does not know his master's business. I call you friends, because I have made known to you everything I have learned from my Father. You did not choose me, no, I chose you: and I commission you to go out and to bear fruit, fruit that will last. And then the Father will give you anything you ask him in my name."

Thus, Jesus sent his disciples out into the world to tell *all* about the new covenant between God and those who follow Christ's teachings, as relayed from the Father. They must conduct their lives with a personal relationship with Jesus and follow his teachings (and therefore God), in order to accomplish salvation and everlasting life.

Jesus promised that when he would no longer be on earth in physical form, the Holy Spirit would provide guidance and be the conduit for the will of God. He charged the disciples to scatter and testify to *all* people their knowledge of His teachings and miracles, so that *all* people might believe and be saved. As Jesus prayed the last time for his disciples, John 17:20-25 says that He also prayed for all who would become believers in his message.

> "My prayer is not for them alone (the disciples). I pray also for those who will believe in me through their (the disciples) message, that all of them may be one, Father, just as you are in me and I am in you. May they also be in us so that the world may believe that you have sent me. I have given them the glory that you gave me, that they may be one as we are one: I in them and you in me. May they be brought to complete unity to let the world know that you sent me and have loved them even as you have loved me. Father, I want those you have given me to be with me where I am and to see my glory, the glory you have given me because you loved me before the creation of the world. Righteous Father, though the world does not know you, I know you, and they know that you have sent me. I have made you known to them and will continue to make you known in order that the love you have for me may be in them and that I myself may be in them."

This long, complicated passage seems to say that God's love for Jesus, His son manifested in human form, will now be relayed to *all* people by the disciples who were chosen by Jesus. *All* who follow the teachings will be one with God.

Thereafter, Jesus was arrested while praying in the garden of Gethsemane, having been betrayed by one of his own disciples. Judas Iscariot, who came with a group of soldiers and officials from the chief priests and Pharisees, signaled to them that Jesus was the one they wanted by kissing him on his cheek, a greeting reserved for friends.

Jesus was taken to the Sanhedrin where he was accused of blasphemy because when questioned, Jesus admitted to being the Christ, the Son of the Almighty One. He was then taken to the Roman governor of Judea, Pilate, to be tried.

Pilate could find no reason to charge him with a crime worthy of execution; but the Jews continued to call for crucifixion on the basis of Jesus's claim that he was a king, even though not of this world. Finally, Pilate relented and turned Jesus over to the Roman soldiers who carried out the will of the Jews and took him out to be crucified with common criminals.

Even as he was being crucified, one of the criminals acknowledged belief in Jesus as the Savior, and was promised a place with Jesus in Paradise.

The New Testament writings record that just as Jesus had described to his disciples, after three days, he overcame death and appeared to his disciples as well as to his mother Mary and friend, Mary Magdalene, all of whom were overjoyed when they saw him.

Then Jesus said to them, "All authority in heaven and on earth has been given to me. Therefore, go and make disciples of all nations, baptizing them in the name of the Father and of the Son and of the Holy Spirit, and teaching them to obey everything I have commanded of you. And surely, I will be with you always, to the very end of the age" (Matthew 28:18-20.)

In John 21:15, Jesus questioned Simon Peter: "Do you love me?" Upon Peter's repeated assurance that he did, Jesus said to him, "Feed my lambs." (Tell the good news to all!)

Jesus left the earth in the year 33CE. At the time of his coming and during his life, the Roman Empire reigned politically within the entire Mediterranean world. Yet the once-dominant Greek culture and their intellect continued to have a major influence during those times.

The Early Christian Church

The Greek philosophy had evolved to a belief of the reality of an eternal spiritual immortality of the soul rather than merely a temporal, material and physical existence. Christianity was in line with that concept and the Romans of the time, who were an inclusive civilization with a sense of solidarity and unity of all mankind under their political organization, did not oppose the new Christian theology. Roman citizenship was frequently granted to non-Romans and by law, honored individual dignity and the right to justice for all people. This sense of unity of mankind under Roman universal law created a favorable setting for belief in a gospel that offered salvation for the repentance of sin.

Subsequently, the Christian church was made a part of the universal Roman establishment. The Romans, who also had developed a superior system of roads radiating out from the Roman forum to every part of the empire, made travel of that day relatively easy. Roads were safe and facilitated the travels of Paul and others to spread the word of Christ and the newly formed Christian Church. One universal language throughout the Empire also made it easy to preach Christ's teachings.

The task for the disciples, who were now empowered by Jesus Christ and guided by the Holy Spirit, was to witness to others that the earthly presence of God through Christ and faith in Christ's word would redeem them from their sins. Christ was the conduit for humanity to God. In believing in Christ, and the sacrifice of his life for the salvation of mankind, humanity was reconciled.

The disciples, as well as Jesus, were Jews and their witness to the Jews was to be a priority; but the Gentiles were to be included as well. When visiting a new city, the synagogues were the first to be visited and many Jews were converted. There was rapid growth of the new Christian church even within the city of Jerusalem and Christian communities were ones of love for one another and genuine equality without social barriers. Jew or Gentile, gender, race and status were of no importance and early Christians evoked tranquility, simplicity and joy in their daily lives.

But there was also much opposition among the Jewish ecclesiastical authorities who may have recognized that Christianity was a threat to their positions. That risk led them to aggressively combat it. The Sanhedrin actively persecuted those who preached Christianity and forbade them to continue. Stephen was the first Christian martyr who was stoned to death when he denounced the Jewish leaders for their rejection of Christ. Of the disciples of Jesus, many were either killed or imprisoned.

Peter is credited with bringing the gospel officially to the Gentiles and those forced to leave Jerusalem continued to spread the word, which resulted in a large Gentile Christian church in Antioch (in Syria). It was in Antioch where the main center of Christianity established itself and where the convert Paul began his ministry. Paul traveled throughout the Mediterranean area establishing and then supporting, through letters and visits, the rapidly increasing number of Christian churches within the Roman Empire.

By the end of the first century, the New Testament had been written and provided accounts of the four gospel writers, Matthew, Mark, Luke, and John. The gospels related their personal relation-ship with Jesus during his time on earth. Theologians feel it is highly unlikely that the actual writing of the gospels was by the disciples themselves, rather it is believed the leaders of the Christian churches that each disciple had founded wrote them. After the first century, the number of Christians increased remarkably—both converted Jews and Greek Gentiles.

Trouble began when Christians refused to offer worship to the Roman emperor, professing spiritual loyalty only to Christ. Christians also worshiped their God quietly and somewhat secretly rather than openly with idols or symbolic manifestations such as was common with the worship of pagan gods during this time throughout the Roman Empire. There were rampant rumors and misunderstandings concerning the meaning of the body and blood of Christ, which led to accusations of cannibalism and other unnatural behaviors. Christians upheld the equality of all people, which led to contempt by the aristocratic segment of Roman society. The occurrence of local calamities as well as problems within the empire as a whole led Roman leaders to single out Christians as a particular threat to the state because of their rapid growth and their seemingly separatist behavior.

As political disorder within the Roman Empire increased, freedom of thought, including religious freedom, became less tolerable until there resulted a ban of Christian meetings, destruction of copies of the Scriptures, and an order for Christians to sacrifice to pagan gods or to be punished with loss of property, exile, imprisonment and even execution by sword or by wild beasts.

But Christianity continued to evolve despite the attempts of the Roman state to abolish it and the new religion became threatened by growth so rapid that converts—Gentiles (Greek), converted Jews, and Romans—developed differences in the Christian doctrine and the precise meaning of Christ's words. Greek interpretation of the writings dealt with philosophical matters while Roman concerns were those of organization and governing doctrines.

The new church sought to develop an authoritative statement of beliefs with a canon or an established tenet of the New Testament. Many now studied the Scriptures in order to develop a true, clear theological meaning. Augustine of Hippo was one who made major contributions to this end and was responsible for the creation of a Christian philosophy and doctrine that was to be carried out by church leaders. The logical choice for this leadership was the bishop of Rome since

Christ, himself, had proclaimed Peter to be the "rock" of his church and the clear instructions "to feed my sheep". Peter was indeed the first "bishop" of Rome and led the way for the development of the papacy to lead the Roman Church. The doctrine developed was to be applied universally to the church as a whole, the so-called catholic church, which literally means "universal" church. It was at this time the beginning of the third century, that the emperor Constantine found favor with the developing Christian church and sought to use it as an ally to maintain a stable state.

Although he declared freedom of worship for all citizens, the Christian community particularly welcomed his edict. With this new decree, Constantine subsidized the church, exempted clergy from public service, banned soothsaying, and formally set apart the "Day of the Sun" (Sunday) as a day of rest and worship. This led to a period of extensive building of Roman basilica-style churches with the structural form of the cross.

The Holy Roman Church—the Papacy

Constantine also founded the city of Constantinople where he shifted the empire's center of political power, leaving the Bishop of Rome with political power as well as spiritual power in the western empire. The Roman Bishop, in fact, became the most powerful individual in the western empire and was acknowledged as Papas (father) from which the term "Pope" was derived.

During the Dark Ages, which began in the fourth century and continued until 1066 CE, the Roman Empire declined and decayed from within, leading many individuals to renounce society and worldliness. Many chose instead to lead a life of solitude and to achieve holiness by contemplation and asceticism. This was the era of monasteries and cloisters, a counterculture that saw the establishment of many different orders of friars and monks.

The Franciscans (St. Francis of Assisi), Benedictines, and Dominicans were some of the more recognizable orders that began during this time. Their role was officially that of converting pagans to Christ; but they are also credited with keeping scholarship and education alive during the Dark Ages when barbarians took over the Roman Empire.

Monks copied and often translated classic manuscripts that would have otherwise been lost, and monasteries and cloisters became safe havens for society's outcasts and travelers in need of help. Even hospitalization and care for the sick were provided as well as a refuge for world-weary men and women.

The papacy was temporarily moved to Spain in the 13th century, after a short stint in France. This transfer of the papacy to Spain was a partnership with the Roman Catholic Spanish nation-state, where it was reasoned that the presence of the papacy in Spain would serve to protect the Roman Catholic Church from the threat of a Muslim invasion into the Iberian Peninsula from north Africa and Morocco after Sicily, the Holy Land and Palestine were converted to Islam. (Mohammed's birth in the sixth century introduced a new religious movement that began in the Middle East and like Christianity, spread rapidly and sought to increase its converts.)

The Crusades

The emperor Constantine residing in Constantinople (the Eastern Roman Empire of Byzantium), was also embroiled in preventing the spread of Islam, which had now taken over the Holy Land and threatened a Muslim takeover of Constantinople. Constantine issued a call for the Crusades to regain the Holy Land. That call was answered from the western empire with hundreds of thousands of crusaders traveling eastward to fight Islam. Meanwhile, the Pope, now alone in Rome, gained more and more authority and with every barbaric tribe being converted to Christianity, their allegiance was directed to Rome rather than Constantinople.

The Pope evolved to be more powerful than the emperor and his influence was such that he could take land from the citizenry, levy taxes for the benefit of the Roman Church and demand total control and obedience over not only the church but also the Roman state. An argument grew that the papacy was God-appointed as the true successor of Peter and it authorized dominion over all kings and emperors.

The pope became a Christ-like figure and exercised divine rights. The decisions and actions of succeeding popes moved further and further away from the New Testament Scriptures and more and more toward the individual power of the Pope both politically and financially.

With the influx of barbarian Christian converts who were accustomed to worshiping pagan gods and idols, images such as statues, angel-likenesses, crucifixes and pictures, as well as devotional rituals, were introduced to help the untutored and uneducated in their worship. During this time the Veneration of Mary, mother of Jesus, also took place.

The Separation of the Roman and Eastern Church—the Great Schism

Over time, with the conversion of the Saxons, Franks and Vikings [European tribes], the concerns of the Western Roman Church and that of the Eastern Church, which was centered in Constantinople and concerned with the spread of Islam, were different. As a result, the Great Schism occurred with the separation of the East and West churches. This separation remains to this day with important and lasting differences.

Although the Roman Church and the Orthodox Church share the same sacraments and teaching authority, the Orthodox Church is less focused on detailed dogma as interpreted by Roman Bishops. The Eastern Church is also more tolerant of views from their Church's directorial constituents whose focus is salvation for the Church and its members.

The Eastern Orthodox Church has no pope and although the clergy administer the sacraments and teach religious matters, their positions as clergy are somewhat at the will of the laity, considering the Church's lay individuals collectively as having a greater ability to prevent error in theoretical religious dogma. The Roman Church, on the other hand, considers their hierarchy of Bishops' collective judgment to be authoritarian and protected by the Holy Spirit. The Roman Church believes that mystical experiences i.e. ecstatic, rapturous feelings of incite into Truth are not within the realm of human life, but the Orthodox encourages its members to pursue these practices.

At the time of the Great Schism, the Spanish Inquisition had taken place; led by the Dominicans as directed by the Roman pope. It demanded that both Jews and Muslims be Christian or be exiled or slaughtered if they held on to their own beliefs.

Those events and arguments over the organization and governance of the church, its ritualistic vestitures, sacraments, and the increasing power of the popes, resulted in a degradation of the papacy. Because of the unchecked power in Rome that had accrued while the emperor was distracted during the battle against Islam at the doorstep of Constantinople, there occurred increasing corruption of the papacy, morally as well as monetarily.

The Roman Church and the Renaissance

Church and state were completely intertwined as justified by "divine right". The power of the church became free of any secular control, which allowed the church to levy taxes when needed or to take land from the citizenry in order to gain control and jurisdiction over territories where there were newly converted Christians. Since many of the newly converted were uneducated, they required comprehensive direction as well as subjugation to the church in all matters—not only of spirituality, but also in daily living.

By the early fifteenth century, well into the Renaissance, an awakening to culture, literature and art occurred, and business and trade blossomed with it. The love of beauty abounded, and the considerable wealth gained from business and trade enabled not only leisure for study, but it also enabled, by the act of patronages, for the rising of a middle class of scholars and artists to make life more pleasant and comfortable.

Lorenzo de 'Medici and his merchant family provided many commissions to scholars and artists. The love of literature and the arts occurred within the papacy also and unfortunately took precedence over spiritual functions. Eventually, this led to a split between man's religion and his daily life. The dogmas of the church were still accepted, and the rituals of religion practiced, but the result was a division between the spiritual and the secular.

Ultimately, with this cultural and concurrent philosophical awakening came the recognition by the citizenry of the misplaced power of the Roman Church. An idea took form that religion should be more personal to the individual and not something carried out only by the clergy for the benefit of the clergy.

The Reformation

Martin Luther and John Calvin became leaders of a religious reformation even though the movement began earlier in various places during the Renaissance. John Wycliffe: England; John Hus: Bohemia; the Italian monk Savonarola; are some noteworthy examples of men who not only objected to papal taxation, but wanted to personalize religion and return to the ideals of the New Testament.

This revival sought to reinstitute Christ as the head of the church rather than the papacy. To support these beliefs, the Bible needed to be available to the people and Wycliffe and others translated Latin manuscripts so that they might be distributed to the common people. The advent of mass printing allowed not only communication to spread far and wide but provided translated scripture (the Gutenberg Bible) for the citizenry.

These forerunners of reformation were, not surprisingly, met with distain and condemnation from the Roman Church. Wycliffe was forced to retire to his rectory, Hus was burned at the stake and Savonarola was hanged for defaming the pope. But gradually, the reformation caught on and spread throughout Europe. John Calvin's theology emphasized the centrality of God in spiritual matters and he advocated personal education for the faithful. He wrote extensively both sermons and commentaries on the books of the Bible.

Famously, Martin Luther, a learned theologian and a witness to the corruptions of Rome, was particularly angered over the practice of indulgences that allowed official forgiveness of sin by the pope for a payment of cash without sincere repentance of that sin.

The practice of indulgences raised proceeds for such things as buildings (St. Peter's Cathedral in Rome, for example) or perhaps for private use by the pope including patronages to the arts or lavish living. Luther wrote and posted *Ninety-five Theses* regarding abuses of the Roman church.

Protestantism

As the centrality of God in religious life gained credence and caused protests over the "divine" leadership of the papacy, the movement became known as the Reformation or Protestantism (from the word protest). Reformation occurred throughout Europe—Scandinavia, Scotland, Ireland, Holland and Flanders—but, also in England where King Henry VIII, who wanted to remarry, was denied a divorce by the pope. Henry therefore proclaimed himself the head of the church in England and thus a reformation of sorts also resulted in a separation from the papacy.

Once this change was initiated, despite a short return to Catholicism by Henry's devout Catholic daughter Mary, the citizenry remained steadfast to the idea of the Reformation. Protestantism returned with Elizabeth I of England (Henry's daughter with Ann Boleyn). She was born in a marriage that followed a divorce not ratified by the pope and for her self-preservation as Queen, she again proclaimed herself supreme head of church and state.

The pope, because of her actions, formally excommunicated her. To Elizabeth I's credit, she retained leadership in matters of the state and although officially head of the church, she turned the operation of the church over to the Church of England whose leaders took thirty-nine articles to Parliament as the creed of the Anglican Church. All clergy were required to follow that creed and it continues to this day.

By this time, most of Europe north of the Alps, with the exception of Spain (to the south), had become part of the Reformation. The pope sought the help of Spain to bring England and hopefully others back into the fold but again, politics and religion comingled. England fought the Spaniards and eventually defeated the famed Spanish Armada, which gained the English control of the seas and finally relieved England 's Protestantism from the Roman threat.

Coinciding with these challenges, there was a rising unrest among the Puritans who felt the Anglican Church was too similar to the Roman Church and sought to change the Episcopal State Church

(Anglican) to that of a Presbyterian (John Knox) or Congregational (John Calvin) church. Thus, Protestant denominationalism began to take root and sought to supersede a state church of reformation. This was certainly not something the monarchy desired, as this meant they would no longer have any control at all of that aspect of English citizenry.

But, the concept of denominationalism agreed with the centrality of God, rather than the papacy, as an important aspect of the church and, whereas Luther's thesis mainly challenged the Roman church's abuses, John Calvin proposed the separation of church and state with the Bible as the only source of instruction. The participation of the congregation during worship was also important for Calvin's Congregationalists. Calvin's system of theology had as its basis that churches should be free from state control.

John Knox of Scotland was dedicated to the "word of God" with the doctrines based solely on Scripture. He, however, championed church governance that was representative and democratic, particularly in the development of the church doctrine. Throughout the reformed northern Europe, Scandinavia, England and Scotland, there was a continuance in the gain of Protestant converts, but with differing denominations depending upon local beliefs.

Roman Church Reform

Meanwhile, a Roman Catholic reform was necessary to combat the losses due to the Protestant reformation. Priests took on missionary roles to regain and expand Catholicism by refocusing on charity, social service and the saving of souls. This was accomplished by orders of brothers such as the Jesuits, Dominicans, and Franciscans who took oaths of poverty, chastity, and complete obedience to the pope. Their function was that of education, fighting heresy, and recruiting converts to Catholicism through foreign missions. Even though the corruption of the papacy had also been reformed, the Roman church sanctioned two methods of coercion to accomplish the goal of combating the Reformation—the Inquisition and an *Index of Books*.

During the Inquisition, any suspected heretic was presumed guilty until they were able to prove their innocence. As a result, subjects of inquiry could be tortured until they confessed and then punished by taking their property or burning them at the stake.

Meanwhile, the development of printing, which helped the Protestants to disseminate their ideas, helped the Roman Church as well. The Roman Church issued a list of books (*Index of Books*) that the faithful were not permitted to read. Among the prohibited books were Protestant editions of the Bible.

The Reformation resulted in an end of control by one universal church—the Roman Church. It was replaced by a series of national state churches in Protestant countries. The Lutherans dominated in Germany and Scandinavia, Calvinism in Switzerland, Scotland, Holland, France, Bohemia and Hungary. England had its Anglican state church and a more radical group, the Anabaptist who believed in the necessity of rebaptism by immersion as well as a complete separation of church and state.

The Anabaptists had a strong presence in Holland, northern Germany and Switzerland. Although there were many doctrinal changes during the Reformation, many of the previous ecumenical creeds were still accepted. However, the belief of salvation by faith with doctrine based solely in the Scriptures was paramount.

The assertion of the importance of an individual's personal relationship with God, which was clarified and given insight by preaching, became the model. The church, any church, was not the final authority, but rather the Scriptures, and their interpretations. The Reformation led to the need for education that enabled individuals to read the Bible for themselves or to study theology in order to assist others in their understanding.

The Reformation, because of its emphasis on education, is credited with stimulating the rise of empirical science and a capitalistic system of commerce. In a religious sense it was certainly responsible for its impact on the Roman Catholic Church that was forced to reform its morals. By 1648, in addition to the Roman Catholic Church, most denominations of the Christian religion had been established.

Christianity in the New World

Although some settlers such as the Puritans of England and the Congregationalists arrived in North America seeking religious freedom, many groups were sent to settle in the Americas to benefit their mother country. They came to acquire land, to establish a presence, to meet the Spanish threat in the new world, to convert the Native Americans and/or to extend Christ's dominion.

Companies, such as the Virginia Company, chartered settlers to Jamestown to set up the Anglican Church. The Massachusetts Bay Company brought the Congregationalist Puritans. Other groups that found their way to the new world were the Baptists who were a separatist outgrowth of the Anglicans, the Quakers, the Methodists, the Mennonites, the Presbyterians and later the Mormons.

Although Catholicism had little presence in the thirteen original colonies, it did arrive in areas that later became Quebec, Louisiana, Florida, New Mexico, Arizona, and California. Native Americans in most areas were gathered and their land absconded while they were forced to convert to Christ's church.

After the colonies and settlements were established, it became a priority to develop an educational system for the colonists so that, as the Reformation demanded, an individual could read his own Bible and so that church and state leaders could be trained. The Bible had its place in the curricula from primary through university learning in centers of advanced learning such as Harvard, William and Mary, Yale, and Princeton. Vocational education was provided through apprenticeships.

With the American Revolution, the colonial churches took different stances in regard to the revolution. Some remained loyal to the English, others to the new world. Because of pacifist beliefs, such as those of the Quakers, Mennonites and Moravians, some remained non-participants. The outcome of the Revolution however, had an important impact on religion with the writing of the Constitution.

The First Amendment officially established the right to freedom of religion and the separation of church and state. Denominations were able to set up national organizations to create national sects of churches such as the Methodist Episcopal Church, the Protestant Episcopal Church, the Presbyterian Church, Dutch Reformed, German Reformed, etc. Individuals were free to choose which church they wished to affiliate with and which doctrine best suited their individual beliefs.

Today, although there are greater than nine-hundred divisions within Protestantism, eighty-five percent of Protestants are split across twelve denominations with differences ranging from fundamentalist, conservative, evangelical, mainline, charismatic and even social activist. Yet all are defined by an individual's personal relationship with God—a faith and trust and the desire to understand the will of God for oneself and to earn God's redeeming love through action.

CHRISTIAN HOLIDAYS

Christianity came about during the Roman Empire at a time when pagan festivals had influence. Many of today's Christian holiday customs carry with them some pagan influence. Most likely this is because early Christians participated in Roman state festivals with the exception of holidays sanctifying the Roman emperor, which they refused to do since they believed that Christ alone should be worshipped. That refusal to pay homage to the emperor eventually resulted in the persecution of Christians.

Pagan events probably affected the actual dates of Christian events, most notably the birth of Jesus that may have been in the month of September on our modern calendar rather than December 24-25th. It's important to remember that Jesus did not define Christian holidays during his time on earth. His preaching was that of a rabbi who taught the Mosaic Law. The liturgical calendar divides the Christian year into seasons with theological emphasis, which for many sects defines the vestments of the clergy, the colors of church adornments and decorations, the scripture readings, and the themes for preaching.

Advent

The liturgical year begins with Advent, which literally means "arrival" or "coming"—the time *before* Jesus' birth and the angels' visits to Elizabeth (mother of John the Baptist) and Mary, the mother of Jesus in preparation for their births. Some Christians today also consider this a time to reflect on the return of Christ and the end of time when those who receive salvation by their belief in Christ will be taken up to dwell with God.

The advent season begins three Sundays before Christmas and continues until Christmas Eve. An advent wreath, traditionally made of evergreens, has four candles that are sequentially lit, one on each of the three Sundays before Christmas. The fourth candle is lit on Christmas Eve. Each candle lighting has a corresponding Scripture reading from the gospel of Matthew, referencing the pending birth of Jesus and how Mary and Joseph were forced to travel for a census and had no place to stay when the birth of Jesus became eminent. In recent years, an Advent calendar has also become a popular addition to the season, especially for children. The calendar dates are covered and each day during the month of December, the day's cover is peeled away or opened as a tiny door for a "surprise" message or picture.

Christmas Eve and Christmas Day

Scripture for these days detail the search for an Inn for Mary and Joseph and the ultimate humble birthplace for the baby Jesus in a manager among the innkeeper's domestic animals. It describes the astrological event of the Star of Bethlehem that led the shepherds tending their flocks to follow the star to a place of extraordinary importance. The scriptures describe the visit of wise men who brought gifts for the much-prophesized birth of the savior of the world.

Of all the Christian holidays, Christmas, the birth of Jesus the Savior of the world, is the most celebrated as a time of joy and hope throughout a history of travail and suffering. This babe of the lineage of David, through his father Joseph and with the purity of his mother Mary, came into the world with the humblest of beginnings as the incarnation of God (God in human form). Millions of representations of this event alone, from the paintings of the Renaissance to the Eastern Orthodox icons, repeatedly remind Christians of the importance of this event.

The custom of gift giving during the Christmas season is presumed to be from the example of the wise men who brought gifts of riches to the newborn babe who had been prophesized centuries before. Another explanation is that this birth is God's ultimate gift to the world and His new covenant for a sinful world.

Others maintain the giving of gifts is of a more secular, commercial origin. Christmas trees, Christmas lights and other decorations are thought by some to be outward symbols and expressions of joy regarding the occasion of the birth of Jesus; however, in truth, they are most likely the remnants of pagan festivals.

Epiphany

This is a day set aside to commemorate the recognition by the wise men of the divinity of the baby Jesus in human form. It is most often illustrated as the "Adoration of the Magi" where the infant Jesus is seen with a halo surrounding his head and his hand raised in the sign of benediction (blessing). Magi is a term describing a Zoroastrian priest from a pre-Islamic monotheistic ancient religion originating in Persia with beliefs in a supreme Lord, free-will, heaven and hell and many of the same tenets that the Judaic religion had at the time of Jesus' birth.

For the days after Epiphany until Lent, the liturgical readings of the scripture focus on Christ's earthly ministry including the miracles he performed. Of note, in the Eastern Orthodox Church, along with icons illustrating the Christ child with a halo surrounding his head, Epiphany focuses on the baptism of Christ when it was publicly revealed that he was indeed the Son of God.

Lent

The season of Lent begins on Ash Wednesday, when burned Palm branch ashes are used to make a cross of blessing on the foreheads of the faithful. It occurs forty days before Easter and is done in remembrance of Christ's time of temptation in the desert after his baptism. Lent continues until Easter Sunday and it's a time of fasting, penitence and remorse for the sinful ways of mankind.

During this solemn time, there is no feasting or celebration and crucifixes and images of saints are often covered. It is customary for the faithful to give up something of importance to them during this time in order to experience sacrifice, if only in a superficial manner as compared to the sacrifice of the life of Christ for man's redemption.

Holy Week beginning with Palm Sunday:

On this day, Jesus rode into Jerusalem on the back of a donkey—an animal symbolizing peace—rather than a horse, which often symbolizes war. Throngs of people waved palm branches, also a symbol of peace, to greet him. They laid their garments on the road to honor his arrival and cheered him along his way. He was greeted like a King. This day, as mentioned earlier, was prophesized centuries before and recorded in the book of Zachariah 9:9.

> "Rejoice greatly, O Daughter of Zion! Shout, Daughter of Jerusalem! See, your king comes to you, righteous and having salvation, gentle and riding on a donkey, on a colt, the foal of a donkey."

The symbolism of his triumphant arrival indicated the claim of Jesus as that of a King in the Kingdom of God, all of which angered the Sanhedrin and subsequently led to his death when the Sanhedrin charged him with blasphemy in the Roman courts.

Christians celebrate Palm Sunday with joy and thanksgiving for the fulfillment of the Old Testament prophecy and to acknowledge Christ as King of the Kingdom of God on earth. Today processions with palm branches or small crosses made from palm fronds are customary. If palm branches are not available, other branches are substituted. On this day in the Roman Catholic faith, First Communion is often given to children after preparatory instruction that has occurred in the prior weeks and months.

Maundy Thursday

Jesus gathered his twelve disciples together to relay to them what would happen to him during the next days. He arranged for them to eat dinner together in an upper room and it was here that he authorized them to witness all that they had seen and all they were taught during their time with him. He charged them to spread his word among all peoples, Jew and Gentile.

Finally, Jesus administered the first Holy Communion when he broke bread to symbolize his broken body and poured a cup of wine to represent his blood, which he was about to shed—a sacrifice on behalf of mankind to pay the debt for their sins. With the payment of this debt for mankind, the new covenant was established and all who believed in Jesus as the Son of God and Savior of the world and lived by his teachings, would themselves be saved from everlasting death.

After this last supper, Jesus went to pray in the Garden of Gethsemane taking two of his disciples with him. In the early morning he was arrested, having been betrayed by one of his own disciples, Judas, for forty pieces of silver, perhaps a symbol of man's earthly temptation and desire for riches over righteousness. Jesus was taken to the Sanhedrin who found him guilty of sacrilege for claiming that he was a king—although of the Kingdom of Heaven. The Sanhedrin delivered him to the Roman Court of Pontius Pilot, who after questioning him, found him to be innocent of the charges. Under duress and protest however, Pilot ultimately turned Jesus over to be crucified with two common criminals.

Good Friday

After being scourged and mocked, Jesus was forced to carry a cross to the place of crucifixion where he was nailed to that cross and suffered an excruciating death. A rich man, Joseph of Arimathea, asked for the body of Christ, which he had wrapped in linen cloths with spices and placed in his own tomb before positioning a large rock in front of the opening to seal it. This day is known as the Passion and is the most somber of all Christian holidays with the liturgy of the crucifixion read from the book of John.

Easter

On this day, a Sunday, and two days after the crucifixion of Jesus, the resurrection of Jesus is celebrated. On Sunday morning, the tomb was found to be empty when his mother Mary and Mary Magdalene went to it to grieve. The tomb was open, the linens laid aside and the body gone. Death had been overcome. Christians often celebrate with a sunrise service of joy at the good news that Jesus lives again and because of his sacrifice, believers are assured to do the same.

The joyousness of the day coincides with annual pagan celebrations of fertility and spring. Hence "Easter" eggs, which represent fertility, are colored with dyes and there is a joyous celebration proclaiming renewed life.

Pentecost

From the time the tomb of Jesus was found to be empty, Jesus, arisen from the dead, appeared in person to many of his disciples as well as to his mother Mary and his friend, Mary Magdalene. The time came however, when Jesus permanently departed from the earthly realm and ascended into heaven to once again be one with the Father God. This occasion was forty days after Easter Sunday and the resurrection of Jesus.

Pentecost of the New Testament coincided to the day of Shavuot, a feast of the Jews of the Old Testament celebrating the giving of the Law to Moses at Sinai. The disciples and other believers in Christ gathered to celebrate this Jewish holiday in the Upper Room where previously they had gathered with Jesus on the evening before his death.

Acts 2:1-2 tells us, "And when the day of Pentecost was fully come, they were all with one accord in one place. And suddenly there came a sound from heaven as of a rushing mighty wind, and it filled all the house where they were sitting."

This was the descent of the Holy Spirit, who would be their comfort and guide, as Christ had promised, after his earthly time ended. This event has been described as the "Birthday of the Church" when the apostles would experience God through the Holy Spirit and spread the word and teachings of Christ to all mankind. This feast is also called Whitsunday particularly in the United Kingdom.

Summary and Comments

Jesus was born, lived, and preached the last three years of his life with the intent to revive the Mosaic laws and to be a divine example of how mankind should strive to live in love and peace. The event was prophesized long before his coming. The timing was crucial as the Jews had been living in a state of desperation under Roman rule for over a century and they had become lax in their observance of the holy code delivered to Moses on Mount Sinai.

Jesus came not only to demonstrate right-living to the Jews; but, also God's compassion for all of humankind. Jesus taught the Talmud, but in fresh and relevant ways. As he went about teaching, he healed the sick and performed miracles, but always with a humble demeanor, attributing the acts to be from God who was a God of compassion and love.

Although Jesus was a Jew and his disciples were also Jews, his teachings and deeds were not only for the Jews, but for *all* people. Jesus was a man like those he ministered to, but he was divine and acquired a bodily form so that he might have relevance to mankind.

People responded to him; they came in droves to wherever he was, pressing upon him until at times he had to preach from a boat at the shores of the Sea of Galilee. The uniqueness of his messages was that it was never about him. It was about God and His great love for mankind. Jesus came to earth to be an example of how God intended humans to live, loving one another and treating others as one would want to be treated themselves rather than the old way of "an eye for an eye".

In the Sermon on the Mount, Jesus revealed to people what traits they should strive for to be blessed by God and he gave them the Lord's Prayer, which included the phrase: *"Thy kingdom come, Thy will be done, on earth as it is in Heaven."* He taught it was God's desire to establish a sacred place of peace and good will on earth for all people to dwell, just as He had originally intended in the Garden of Eden,.

There was the matter of sin however; the actions of men that separate them from God. In this regard, Jesus preached loving kindness, forgiveness, loving one's enemies, and resolving one's own misdeeds before pointing out another's. He emphasized the importance of acknowledgement and sorrow for one's transgressions. By following these principles and living as Jesus demonstrated during his time on earth, the relationship with the Almighty can be reestablished.

When Jesus was crucified, died, and was resurrected, there was concrete proof that death could be overcome by being obedient to God. For, as Jesus taught, God is compassionate and loving and forgives man's sins when a person is sincerely regretful for committing them.

When Jesus' earthly time ended, the third coeternal part of the Holy Trinity, the Holy Spirit, was sent to his followers who were to carry on his earthly work. Jesus, as God in human form, and the Holy Spirit are points of contention particularly with the Jews who did not become followers of Christ. They argued that God can only be one, not three entities, and that the trinity indicates polytheism, not monotheism. A real-world counter argument is that of the metaphor of water, which exists in three forms—ice, liquid and steam—yet all are chemically the same: H_2O.

In Jerusalem, in the same upper room as the Last Supper, Christ appeared after his resurrection and instructed his disciples to go out into the world and spread the good news. Until that time, the words and actions of Jesus had not been written down. It was therefore by word of mouth that his teachings were initially dispersed. It wasn't until after the disciples had passed on that the communities associated with them sought to record Christ's teachings from his time on earth. Those writings, the Gospels, along with Paul's letters of assistance in the establishment of Christian churches, as well as other books of the New Testament came about.

Even with the absence of Christ in a physical body, the recruitment to Christianity caught on like wildfire. There was a generalized feeling that a mystical presence of Christ, in the form of the Holy Spirit, continued to guide the new spiritual awakening that taught love and equality for all who believed that this was the way to God's grace. The physical Jesus was now replaced, in the physical realm, by the Church, whose task was to carry on the teachings of Christ in the world in accordance with what he had taught and demonstrated during his time on earth.

It embodied a social code of love and tolerance for others, devotion to God and a pledge to live upright and honorably. By this code for living, those who followed Christ's teachings would, as had Christ, not be conquered by death, but have eternal life.

As the early Church evolved, it transitioned into the Roman Catholic Church led by humans, who by nature are fallible. Over many years, as history has shown, great imperfections became the reality and after more than a thousand years, a protest against this basically human institution finally manifested.

From that protest, (Protestantism) reforms quickly occurred and doctrine reverted to the scripture in lieu of human leadership and interpretations. Since the Bible and the facts of Jesus' life and teachings were written many years after his death, there were variations in precisely what and how humans were to believe and to conduct their lives. This, in turn, led to numerous denominations within the Protestant sect of Christianity. Protestants considered the scriptures, rather than man, to be the most reliable way to interpret and practice the way of life that God wanted his people to live. The Protestant reform subsequently acted as a catalyst for Roman Catholic reforms that then followed.

References/Bibliography

Holy Bible: King James Version.

Holy Bible: New International Version

Alpha News Daily. "Prophecies of the Messiah from the Old Testament—Tanakh". Retrieved February 22, 2016, from

http://www.alphanewsdaily.com/Messiah1.html.

Armstrong, K. (1997). *Jerusalem: One city, three faiths*. New York: Ballantine Books.

Armstrong, K. (1993). *A history of God: The 4,000-year quest of Judaism, Christianity and Islam*. New York: Ballantine Books.

Cairns, E. E. (1996). *Christianity through the centuries: A history of the Christian Church* (3rd ed.). Grand Rapids, MI: Zondervan.

Clarifying Christianity.com. (1998). "Messianic Prophecies: The Bible's predictions about Jesus, written centuries before he was born." Retrieved February 22, 2016, from http://clarifyingchristianity.com/m_prophecies.html.

Cocherell, B.L. (2007). "The coming of the Messiah." Retrieved February 22, 2016,

From http://www.bible-prophecy.net/prophecybook2/b2w17.html.

Deem, R. (2011). "Prophecies of Jesus Christ as Messiah." Retrieved February 22, 2016, from http://www.godandscience.org/apologetics/prophchr.html.

Engelbrecht, E. A. (Ed.). (2013). *Concordia's complete Bible handbook*, Second Edition. St. Louis, Mo: Concordia Publishing.

Hunt, M. (2000). "Isaiah's prophecies of the Messiah fulfilled in Jesus of Nazareth." Retrieved February 22, 2016, from https://www.agapebiblestudy.com/prophecies/Messiah.

Rose Publishing. "Prophecies of the birth of Christ." Retrieved February 22, 2016, from https:bible.org/article/prophecies-birth-christ.

Smith, H. (1991). *The World's Religions.* New York: HarperCollins

Wikipedia contributors. "Mormons." In Wikipedia, The free encyclopedia, Retrieved July 13, 2018, from https://en.wikipedia.org/wiki/s.

Wikipedia contributors. "Liturgical year." In Wikipedia, The free encyclopedia,

Retrieved July 13, 2016, from https://en.wikipedia.org/wiki/Liturgical_year.

Wikipedia contributors. "Pentecost." In Wikipedia, The free encyclopedia, Retrieved July 13, 2016, from https://en.wikipedia.org/wiki/Pentecost.

Wikipedia contributors. "Christianity and Paganism." In Wikipedia, The free encyclopedia, Retrieved July 13, 2016, from https://wikipedia.org/wiki/Christianity_and_Paganism.

ISLAM

Islam is the third of three religions originating from Abraham. With Hagar, Abraham fathered a son Ishmael and eventually, as a test of faith, God commanded Abraham to take Ishmael and his mother to the desert valley near where Mecca stands today and leave them there. Abraham was reluctant, but God convinced Abraham that Hagar and Ishmael would be safe, so he obeyed God and took the mother and child into the desert and left them there with food and water.

Some divergence exists between the Quran and Torah accounts of this incident, as the Torah account proclaims that Ishmael's offspring "would become a great nation" while Islam considers Ishmael a Prophet—the results of Abraham's obedience to God. (Isaac, the son of Abraham and Sarah, remained in Palestine to become the father of the Israelites.)

Well into the sixth century, the people of Arabia remained mostly isolated from one another and felt no obligation to anyone other than their own tribe and family. Their world was chaotic with drunken orgies, gambling, polytheism, no moral constraint and smoldering undercurrents of disagreement that often caused sudden frays and violent blood feuds. The time was right for a deliverer and that deliverer was a descendent of Ishmael, Muhammad ibn Abdullah, who was born in 570 CE. Muhammad tended sheep as a child until he eventually became a manager of caravans.

Muhammad was by nature pure-hearted, of gentle disposition, and had an unusual sensitivity to human suffering. Eventually he married a widow fifteen years older than him who proposed the marriage to him. He remained devoted to her until her death. Khadija was his confidant and she believed wholeheartedly in his integrity. She, too, was a merchant and had successfully traded her goods by caravan, hiring others to travel for her and to negotiate according to her instructions.

Eventually she had cause to hire Muhammad ibn Abdullah to manage her caravan and his integrity impressed her greatly.

At this time, there were few who were contemplatives and fewer still that worshiped one God; Muhammad was one who did and, like Abraham before him, he became convinced Allah was the one true God. He often sought solitude from the chaos of everyday living and regularly pursued the seclusion of a hidden cave on Mount Hira outside of Mecca. Unable to accept the corrupt society of the day, gradually Muhammad's cave visits became more compelling and frequent. During one visit, as had transpired with Abraham, Moses, Samuel, Isaiah and Jesus, a voice from heaven announced, "You are the appointed one," and the angel Gabriel (Jabril) charged Muhammad to "proclaim his experiences and beliefs."

Muhammad was initially shaken, fearful and distressed, thinking of this overwhelming task for which he felt unprepared and incapable. Finally, after confiding with Khadija, she responded, "You will be the Prophet of this people."

From that moment on, Muhammad's life was no longer his own. Thus began the revelation of the Book—the Quran—the words of God, which took a total of twenty-three years to receive and transmit.

Muhammad was extremely modest and humble and he refused to inflate himself into anything more than a mere conveyor of God's word. Initially, there was violent hostility toward his claim of only one God. One reason for this was that Mecca would certainly lose revenue from the many pilgrimages made there to appease all the polytheistic gods. Additionally, the concepts of democratic values and equality that were functions of this new belief challenged the established social order that was fragmented by class distinctions. As a result of this, Muhammad and his few followers were frequently ostracized, pelted with stones, and sometimes physically beaten.

After three years, the newly formed group had only managed to convert about forty followers and Muhammad finally left Mecca to go to Medina where he was better treated and where he became an administrator and statesman who dispensed justice and mercy with the purpose of liberty and order. For the next ten years, he worked unpretentiously to meld the heterogeneous and conflicting tribes, including several Jewish communities, into an orderly confederation. From diversity and sometimes raging conflict, citizens gradually acquired a spirit of cooperation. Word of those accomplishments became known throughout Arabia and Muhammad gained much favor. Despite his successes however, the army of Mecca invaded Medina to overtake it and oust the Muslims.

After several battles, the Muslims overcame the Meccan army and peacefully conquered the whole of the city, which then underwent a mass conversion. It was not in Muhammad's nature to gloat from such a victory, but rather he forgave those who had fought against him. Almost immediately, he went to the Ka'ba, the cubical temple dedicated to Abraham, and with a new focus on Islam, he rededicated it to Allah, the one God.

Eventually, Muhammad returned to Mecca and died two years later in 632CE. At the time of his death, all of Arabia had come together as Muslim. He had succeeded in uniting his countrymen and by the end of the seventh century, his followers had also converted many in Armenia, Persia, Syria, Palestine, Iraq, Northern Africa, and Spain.

Muhammad has been declared by some to be the single most influential person in history with an "unparalleled combination of secular and religious influence." Today, worldwide, there are 1.6 billion Muslims and Islam is the second largest religion on earth.

Muhammad's life included an exceptional range of experiences—shepherd, caravan merchant, hermit, exile, soldier, lawmaker, prophet-priest-king, and mystic. In his personal life he was orphaned as a young child, shepherded sheep, led a caravan and initially, with his marriage to Kadija, had one wife until her death. He was also a bereaved father, a widower, husband of many wives, and in all these roles he was exemplary.

Although Muhammad was illiterate and could barely write his name, through him God's miracle book was revealed. Grammatically the book was perfect and poetic. It became a book memorized in its entirety by many.

The Quran is eighty percent of the length of the New Testament, having 114 chapters or "surahs" arranged in order of decreasing length. Surah 2 has 286 verses; Surah 114 has six verses. It is thought of as God's book, written by God but revealed in Arabic through Gabriel or *Jibril* to Muhammad.

The book was relayed in segments over a period of twenty-three years by a reverberating voice that was said to be that of Gabriel. Muhammad had no control over the revelations, but over time, both his own voice and appearance were changed. By some accounts, it was reported that the words God revealed, "assaulted" him as if weighted, solid and heavy and that when Muhammad passed on the text to be recorded by followers, he appeared to be in a trance-like state.

The Quran is a continuation of the Torah (Christian Old Testament), the Psalms of David, and the New Testament. Christians, Jews, and Muslims were now all "People of the Book". Although the Quran began with the tribal peoples of Arabia, other lands were addressed and validated.

"To every people we have sent a messenger. And when their messenger cometh, it will be judged between them fairly, and they will not be wronged." (Surah X: 48.) "Messengers we have mentioned to thee before, and (some) we have not mentioned to you." (Surah IV: 164.)

The effect of the Quran is greatly embellished by the Arabic language, which is moving, poetic and typically has an irresistible influence over an Arabic reader. The rhythm, melodic cadence and rhyme produce a powerful effect. Translations to other languages may result in a more banal effect and at times may even cause confusion; thus, the Quran's power is not only the literal meaning, but also, the lyrical language. The theme of the Quran is a proclamation of the unity with God whose mercy, omniscience, and omnipotence justifies total dependence of humans on Him—a Lord-servant relationship is the essential point. Within the Quran, God is referred to by ninety-nine different names—"the Merciful One," "the Most Forgiving," etc. God's direct pronouncements act as a repository of truth and a roadmap for living, including maxims for meditation.

The basic underpinnings of Islam are identical to its fore-runners—Jewish and Christian. The exception is that Jesus, who in Christianity is claimed to be the Son of God, is honored in Islam as a prophet and his deification is denied. To the Muslim, there is only one God, that being Allah and the concept of a three-in-one or a tri-une God is negated. Likewise, the reference to God's children is similarly rejected in Islam as this places God into a too-human mode.

Allah is awesome and fear inspiring, powerful, infinite, omnipotent and omnipresent. Although Allah may be seen as a stern and wrathful judge, his compassion and mercy are cited in the Quran 192 times as opposed to seventeen references of wrath and vengeance.

The Arabic word for "infidel", rather than being a term for an "unbeliever", more accurately translates to "one who is ungrateful of Allah's blessings." In fact, Surah II: 256 states:

"Let there be no compulsion in religion. The right direction is henceforth distinct from error. He who has rejected false deities and believeth in Allah hath grasped a firm handhold which will never break." Further, Surah V: 48 "To everyone have We given a law and a way.... And if God had pleased, he would have made one people (of one religion). But he hath done otherwise, that He might try you (judge you) in that which He hath severally given unto you: wherefore press forward in good work. Unto God shall ye return, and he will tell you that concerning which ye disagree."

Pre and post Islam in Arabia witnessed a remarkable moral advance within a short time. There had been inequities in wealth and possessions and inter and intra tribal violence that dominated social interaction. Drunkenness, gambling, female infanticide and general disregard for women made up the moral climate. With the revealed Quran, the laws of morality became explicit and provided a spiritual guide as well.

The Quran was further supplemented by the authoritative *Hadith*, which is based on Muhammad's words, practices and actions. The *Hadith*, which was recorded by Muhammad's followers immediately after his death has been, for the most part, verified to be authentic by a system requiring direct observation of more than one reliable source.

Although some individual sayings and actions attributed to Muhammad in the *Hadith* were found to have originated hundreds of years after his death, overall the *Hadith* is a dependable resource that records Muhammad's example of how to live according to God's commandments. Islam is wholly about brotherly and sisterly love and it joins faith to politics and religion for the benefit of society as a whole. The Quran is mainly focused on God, on creation, mankind and the Day of Judgment. Its emphasis is on human deeds.

The Five Pillars of Faith for Personal Life

It might be suggested that God's revelations to humankind were given in four stages. First, the truth of monotheism—God's oneness—which had begun with Adam, then Abraham, Moses, Jesus and finally Muhammad. The second was the Ten Commandments through Moses. Third, God's revelation of the Golden Rule—"we do to others, as we would have them do to us"—through Jesus. The remaining step was how we should love our neighbor and what deeds and duties God's people should follow in their private life.

The first of Islam's Five Pillars of Faith is the creed and profession of the faith known as the *Shahadah*. It is simple, brief and explicit. "There is no god but God, and Muhammad is His Prophet." It states emphatically that there is only one God; but it also gives legitimacy to Muhammad as well as renders validity to the book Muhammad transmitted. Particularly, the first part of this phrase is repeated multiple times throughout the life of a Muslim during moments of joy or gratitude as well as during times of trouble, danger and tribulation. In Arabic: *"La ilaha illa llah"* is uttered as the ultimate answer to all questions, to all joys, to all dangers.

The second Pillar commands constancy in prayers of thankfulness and for keeping one's life in perspective before the Creator, including submitting one's will to God. The degree of consistency, it turns out, was a negotiation between Muhammad and God.

The story is told that a white steed carried Muhammad to Jerusalem and then upward through the sixth heaven to be face to face with other prophets and God. With the exception of when being in eminent danger, it was decided one should pray five-times a day: at dawn, when the sun is at its zenith, when the sun is at mid-decline, when the sun is setting, and before retiring.

Muslims should pray in mosques when they are able, and Friday noon is a preferred time. Although initially Muslims prayed in the direction of Jerusalem, later Muhammad changed this to Mecca thereby creating the sense of a worldwide fellowship of Muslim prayer.

From Muhammad's practices and teachings, the ritual of prayer includes washing (*wadu*) to purify the body and soul before standing shoulder to shoulder with one another as petitioners. Then, all kneel in unison and touch their foreheads to the ground. In this somewhat humble, fetal position, the prayer is one of rebirth while at the same time presents one's self as small and insignificant in the presence of the Divine.

Charity is the third pillar of Islam. Since disparity of wealth and possessions always exist, those who have more should lift the burden of the less fortunate. Poorer people owe nothing, but those of middle or upper incomes should distribute one-fortieth of their *entire* accumulated wealth. In addition to their income, the value of their possessions should be included to calculate their debt for those in need.

The fourth pillar is that of the observance of Ramadan, which is a month within the Islamic calendar. Ramadan is Islam's holiest month as it is the month Muhammad received his initial revelation and also the time period when the religion was taken from Mecca to Medina. Healthy individuals should fast during the entire month from sunrise to sunset. Food, drink, smoking and sexual activities are prohibited during this time. After sunset, Iftar, a light meal can be eaten and before dawn, Suhoor, another light meal is permitted.

This practice promotes self-reflection and self-discipline as it emphasizes one's frailty and reliance on God. It also fosters compassion: only when hungry can another's plight of hunger be understood.

The fifth pillar is that of a pilgrimage to Mecca—the *hajj*—which will be detailed later. Mecca is the place where the revelation of the Quran was received from God and where the Ka'ba, in honor of the One God Allah, is located. Muslims who are physically and economically able should make the pilgrimage at least once during their lifetime. This practice brings together people from around the world, which fosters a better understanding of one another.

The Five Pillars are things that Muslims should do; there are also things they should *not* do. Some of the forbidden behaviors include murder, thievery, lying, eating pork, drinking alcohol, sexual promiscuity, and adultery. All these things are detailed in the Quran.

Islam After Muhammad: Shia and Sunni

Despite the Arab world's strong loyalty for family or tribal origin, Muhammad had succeeded in uniting much of the Arab world in Islam. After his death in 632 CE however, the Muslim community was left without a chosen successor. As was the case before Muhammad, family allegiance became a factor in the assumption by some that a member of Muhammad's direct family should assume his role as caliph.

Ali, Muhammad's beloved cousin and closest relative whom he had mentored and about whom he said: "I am from Ali and Ali is from me; he is the guardian of every believer after me." Those words, to some, seemed to verify Ali as the leader that Muhammad would have wished for. However, other stories give an account of the Prophet's instruction to his followers that they would not choose wrong if they chose the most respected elder to head the community.

Before Muhammad was buried, a *shura*, the traditional inter-tribal forum to reach agreement on issues or disputes, was called. Ali did not attend the *shura*—perhaps because he was preparing the body of the Prophet for burial. Those who were present at the *shura* were mostly Umyyads from Mecca who, after disagreeing on several proposals for caliph, ultimately chose Abu Bakr as their spiritual leader and statesmen. Abu Bakr had been the Prophet's close friend and companion and he had strong support because of his fairness and integrity. He was also Muhammad's father-in-law (from Muhammad's wife Aeisia). Although Muhammad's followers in the *shura* generally agreed upon Abu Bakr, there was opposition by a smaller group of companions who strongly felt the Prophet's close companion, cousin and son-in-law, Ali ibn Abi Talib, was more qualified and should succeed the Prophet as head of the caliphate. Ali, however, did not fight for the position and although all agreed he was devoted to Islam, most present at the *shura* focused their support on Abu Bakr, who was a good compromise in respect to clan rivalries, group politics and personal jealousies.

Ultimately Abu Bakr was accepted as leader and Ali, too, pledged his loyalty. Abu Bakr continued with Islam's expansion, but was eventually struck with a fever and died after only a few years. On his death, Abu Bakr appointed his own successor—his son Omar—to be the second caliph. Omar had also been a close companion to Muhammad and his appointment was quickly settled with Ali acting as his deputy. The years following the death of Muhammad were by many accounts turbulent and full of strife. Ali was dealt yet another blow when Uthman was selected third caliph and although under his caliphate, Islam continued to aggressively spread, the once-close community became unsettled as it grew and rivalries developed.

During the time of the three caliphs (Abu Bakr, Omar and Uthman), Ali remained faithful and was credited with preventing many missteps and mistakes because of his scholarly, calm demeanor. Upon Uthman's death in battle, Ali, at last, became the fourth caliph as well as Islam's first imam or spiritual leader. Ali the intellectual, quiet and cultured warrior, governed according to religious tenants with equalitarian priorities. He was reputed to be a righteous and just caliph. He was however, overwhelmed with the challenges of this unsettled time and was ambushed on his way to the mosque and killed with a sword dipped in poison.

The first four caliphs, Abu Bakr, Omer, Uthman, and Ali, were Muhammad's most trusted and faithful companions and were loyal in carrying out the model of governing and personal behavior that Muhammad had taught and demonstrated to them. After a time however, with the rapidly expanding growth of Islam and the influence of different cultures that were converted, differences arose, and tribal and family allegiances again became significant and disruptive to the cause.

Historically, after Muhammad's death, many conflicting accounts about his successors were recorded. Depending upon the perspective of those who recorded the events of the conclaves to select a caliph, the accounts relayed both satisfaction with the choices and dissatisfaction beginning with that of the first caliph, Abu Bakr. Ali's supporters who were present believed that only Muhammad's progeny should be his successor. They insisted that even though Abu Bakr was the father of Muhammad's beloved wife Aeisha, he was not a blood relative as Ali was.

As time passed, the divisions that developed within Islam became more pronounced—particularly after a battle at Karbala where Ali's son Hussein and his followers were killed, beheaded, and reportedly left unceremoniously to rot on the battleground. Hussein became a martyr and with that particular event, the Shia, or "the group", who believed that only direct, blood relatives of Muhammad should become the head of the community as well as spiritual leader was established. Others, "followers" now denoted as Sunni, did not ascribe to that technicality.

After the slaying of Hussein, the Shia continued to challenge the caliphates with their notion that only the blood kin of the Prophet had the right to rule. The Shia spiritual leaders, the imams, were soon seen as potential threats by Sunnis and were carefully watched. From the seventh Shia imam on, they were kept under house arrest and it has been alleged they were all eventually poisoned. At the time of the twelfth imam, it is believed that Allah physically removed him from earth to preserve his life.

When Allah permits his return, the reappearance of the twelfth imam along with the return of Jesus and Hussein will indicate the end of time and the beginning of perfect justice. This is a clear parallel to the Judeo-Christian prophecies.

The Sunni do not ascribe to this and these differences are often perceived as a threat. The once mere disagreements regarding Islamic practice and theory are now a means for persecution between Sunni and Shia. Sunnism has become about the law while Shiism has evolved to encompass rituals, piety and following the Islamic law as interpreted by those with special knowledge and perceptive interpretation.

The events of Hussein's demise provided the backdrop for Ashoura (Al-'Ashura, the tenth day of the month of Muharram) that continues to take place annually throughout Shia communities and in cities such as Lahore (Pakistan), Luchnow (India), Tehran (Iran), Karbala (Iraq), Bahrain and southern Lebanon.

Processions emerge from various locations to converge into one grand procession, visiting mosques along the way. The procession is led by a young man carrying a staff with strips of red, green and white cloth fluttering from it. At the top of the staff are a black pennant-like flag and a carved hand that represent the five holiest people the Shia regard: Muhammad, his daughter Fatima, his son-in-law and cousin Ali, and his grandsons, Hasan and Hussein. Black flags also mark Shia houses and mosques. Behind the man carrying the staff is a rider-less white horse with a beautiful empty saddle to remind the observers of the murdered Hussein. The crowd greets the horse with adulation and several grieving women follow chanting "O Hussein" as they pray for forgiveness.

On this day, it is believed Allah answers prayers and forgives the sins of penitents. As the procession proceeds, a rhythmic thudding evolves either with beating drums and/or chanting followed by men dressed in black who walk four abreast and beat their chests with both hands while shouting "Ya Hussein!"

The sound of the voices echoes throughout the city and the ritual becomes deeply spiritual, communal and full of symbolism and passion. It is an audible and visual renewal of Shia faith and piety.

Today there is very little difference theologically to distinguish Shiism from Sunnism. There are some small differences in practice as well as some differences in how Islam is interpreted. Sunnism was developed and legitimized from a consensus of the majority; however, Shias do not put much credence into majority opinions in matters of religion. They believe the truth comes from virtuous leadership originating from the Prophet himself and his descendants.

Secondly, while Sunnis believe the Quran can be read and understood by anyone, the Shia believe the sutras and the religion have layers of truth that eventually lead to absolute Truth. They believe the inner meanings may be esoteric and require interpretation by an imam who is thought to be blessed with special knowledge.

Although these differences may be real at some level, for the average Muslim within each sect, they identify as Shia or Sunni most frequently by family ties. However, loyalty to one sect or the other is real and is mostly propagated by political means whereby political parties and candidates who advocate for each sect's cause with support for candidates and leaders based on their identification as Sunni or Shia.

With the establishment of seminaries, libraries and mosques in Iran, there developed an intellectual attribute to Shiism that served to strengthen that sect there. Scholars known as *ulama* were recognized as experts of Islamic sacred law and theology. The esoteric interpretations provided a foundation for a distinct Shia philosophy in Iran. From the *ulama* scholars in religious law, the ayatollahs emerged who eventually replaced the authority of the imams.

The "Karbala factor", as a result of Hussein's martyrdom, became the underpinning for such events as the 1970's revolution against the oppressive Shah of Iran by the exiled Khomeini. Khomeini succeeded in the establishment of a theocracy and the Republic of Iran, declaring himself Supreme Leader, which ultimately became oppressive in its own right.

Wahhabism

Wahhabism emerged on the Arabian Peninsula as a "back to our roots" reformation movement during the eighteenth century. It was founded by Muhammad ibn Abd al-Wahhab, a purist Sunni tribesman. Wahhabism sought to eradicate many practices that had been added over the centuries since the time of Muhammad's death. Anything but the literal reading of the Quran was rejected including any suggested mediation between man and God.

This movement even disregarded Muhammad other than his being the mere messenger of God and the Wahhabis sought to prevent worship of the Prophet by not allowing his birthday to be celebrated and by destroying the Prophet's tomb. Likewise they ignored and disdained Hussein (Shia) and invaded Karbala to desecrate his shrine. A Wahhabi commander, who later became the first King of Saudi Arabia, took particular vengeance on the Shia and, in fact, issued a jihad against all Shia as being enemies of Islam.

Additionally, the cemetery where the Prophet's daughter was buried, as well as the burial sites of several Shia imams, were destroyed. Overall, the presence of Shias in Saudi Arabia since the 1930s, when the Saudi state took form, have been systematically marginalized and regarded as undesirable. Arising from the strict interpretation of the Wahhabi offshoot of Islam came the *mutawaeen*—the morality police—whose task is to enforce and promote virtue and prevent vice.

Resulting Discord

Since the aftermath of Muhammad's death, there has been a long history of not only different outlooks on how Islam should be practiced, but through the years many Muslims acquired a definitive intolerance of those differences.

Although theologically there is little difference in Sunni and Shia Islamic beliefs, mutual distain, prejudice, distrust, and often-violent actions and reactions have resulted. This sustained conflict over the years, and the attempt by each sect to establish their "preferred way" has created intolerance and division.

In any particular locale, individuals who are in the minority are often marginalized and offered few opportunities by "the others" who happen to be in the majority. Or, those perceived to have different Islamic practices may be bullied into following the prescribed local path by sometimes-violent means. This is all done in the name of Islam, but with a hope and goal that their particular Islamic philosophy will achieve recognition and autonomy.

After World War II, further conflict arose with the disintegration of colonial power throughout the Middle East. Territories were parceled off and governments were formed and led by individuals who once served the interests of the colonial nations. Authoritarian, non-democratic regimes were imposed, products of their colonial governances that aimed at a top-down control of the populations rather than protection of the state.

The new states might have been Muslim, but they evolved out of Western influence, often with a Christian and western way of thought.

Secular division of religion and state was inflicted on the newly established governments even though secularism is not prescribed in traditional Islam. With the continued economic and political interests of the west added to this complex situation, the Middle East became and remains a volatile part of the world.

Simply stated, Sunni Islam or offshoots of Sunni exist in the majority of Middle Eastern countries such as Egypt, the Arabian Peninsula, Palestine, Turkey (since Ottoman days) and Jordan. Of note, the royal family of Jordan is Hashemite with King Abdullah a descendant of the Prophet through Muhammad's daughter Fatima and her husband who was Muhammad's son-in-law as well as the Prophet's paternal first cousin. Jordan is Sunni however, despite the fact that it is the Shia who claimed that Islam leadership should be descended from the Prophet's bloodline. Iraq was Sunni under Suddam Hussein, although this region has always had a Shiite majority. (Hussein was empowered by the former British occupants before their departure.) Since his death, there has been a Shia revival because Shia were severely marginalized during the Hussein postcolonial regime. This situation has been a disruptive force throughout the Middle East. Saudi Arabia has settled into Wahhabism, the fundamentalist offshoot of Sunnism.

The Shia focus is on the Quran and its literal interpretation, but it also relies on interpretations by intermediaries who explain deeper meanings of the holy texts. Shia Islam prevails in northern India and Pakistan and the Iraqi cities of Najaf and Karbala, where the mosque and burial site of Hussein is located.

Iran is wholly Shia with a strict and conservative interpretation of Sharia law from the influence of the Ayatollah Kohmeini,
who declared himself to be a *special*, and by some accounts, a messianic messenger.

Shiite Islam is also well established in areas of Africa's east
coast, and by immigration, to some isolated communities in the U.S.
and Canada.

It should be mentioned that in the Middle East, because government and politics are so deeply associated with Islam and the Quran,
political parties are also embedded in the various sects of Islam—both
modern and conservative.

The involvement of post-colonial communism and socialism in
some areas, along with its inflicted religious persecution, has influenced bringing about the Muslim Brotherhood and Hezbollah, which
are examples of political parties that are influential in the current
events of both religious affairs and government.

The Importance of Jerusalem for Islam

During the lifetime of Muhammad, after the revelations from
Allah were transmitted and with the direction received from Allah,
the new branch of religious faith was established and became known
as Islam. Muhammad was declared to be the last prophet of the Judaic-
Christian religions founded by Abraham. After the entire Quran was
received, Muhammad was taken on a white steed through the night
sky to visit Jerusalem and the site of The Dome of the Rock (at the
Temple Mount).

This site is said to be where Adam built the first altar to God and also where Abraham was about to sacrifice his son Ishmael (or Isaac—in the Jewish version) in obedience to God who commanded him to do so. The Dome of the Rock is claimed also to be the site upon which the Jewish King Solomon built his Temple in the 800's BCE, which was later destroyed by the Babylonian King Nebuchadnezzar in 586 BCE when Jerusalem was captured. The second temple built at the same site around 515 BCE was destroyed by the Roman Empire in 70 CE and was said to be a Roman retribution against the Jews they held responsible for the crucifixion of Christ or, by the Jewish account, punishment by God to the Jews for their disobedience to His commandments.

It was on this same site (the Dome of the Rock) that an Islamic caliph built the Al-Asqa Mosque to commemorate where Muhammad was carried on the white steed and from where he ascended into the heavens to meet other prophets—in particular Abraham, Moses, and Jesus.

It was here that Allah commanded one of the Five Pillars of Faith i.e. to pray five times a day. "Glory to He (Allah/God) Who did take His servant for a journey by night from the Sacred Mosque to the farthest Mosque whose precincts We did bless." (Surah XVII: 1.)

For a time after this holy, miraculous visit to Jerusalem, Muslims turned toward Jerusalem during prayer. In 625 CE, the prayer site was changed toward Mecca and the Ka'ba. ".... And now verily We shall make thee turn (in prayer) toward the *qiblah*(direction) which is dear to thee. So turn thy face toward the Inviolable Place of Worship

(Mecca), and ye (Muslims), wheresoever ye may be, turn your faces (when ye pray) toward it. (Surah II:144.)

Islam's Expansion

In the years after Muhammad's death, despite the turmoil of leadership and the divisions it caused, the religion spread quickly throughout the eastern Mediterranean including Syria, Lebanon and Egypt. Although Islam had begun in the Arabian Peninsula and spread throughout the Middle East for those who would be profited by it, it was a faith meant for all humankind even though its purpose was not to seek either Christian or Jewish converts, but rather to include Islamic converts with those who were already "People of the Book".

Islam also spread throughout northern Africa and finally, by 711 CE, across the straits of Gibraltar into Spain where the Berbers and Arabs there were quickly converted. The Moors, as the Spanish Muslims were known, remained intact in Spain for 400 years and in some parts of Spain for 700 years. The Moors were eradicated or exiled during the time of the Christian Inquisition when the Roman church focused its Catholic revival westward after Constantinople lost its position as the eastern center of Christianity.

In the 6th through the 11th centuries, Byzantium had become the center of Christianity with the Roman church centered in Constantinople. During this time, Christians held the view that since God ruled over heaven, the Roman Emperor should rule over earth as a theocracy to embrace the entirety of its people who should therefore all become members of the one true Christian church.

This belief understandably caused a great clash between Christians and Muslims since Islam was now the major religious philosophy in the Middle East and still spreading westward into Turkey toward Constantinople. Jerusalem had become a city of utmost importance for all three Abrahamic religions: the Jews for the Temple Mount, the Christians for the place of Christ's crucifixion and his burial place, the Holy Sepulcher, and Islam for the Al-Aqsa Mosque, where Muhammad ascended into heaven to come face-to-face with Allah and the other prophets.

Each claimed the right to their holy sites and through the ages violent struggles to possess the city itself have resulted. With the Christian belief that their sins would be forgiven if they fought to maintain Christianity in Byzantium and reclaim Jerusalem exclusively for Christendom, there was no shortage of crusaders willing to fight to maintain control of the holy places for the Roman church.

The Crusades were brutal, bloody struggles for both Christians and Muslims, including pillaging and the murder of thousands of Jews by Christians.

History, regardless of whose viewpoint is taken, suggests aggression on both sides—either to control territories where each had religious interests or to proclaim dominance over the other. Even if Islam had not begun with the intent to convert others to their belief or to thwart the beliefs of Christians, the situation certainly lacked understanding from either side. By the 1400's, the Ottoman Muslims finally took over Constantinople for good and eventually laid claim as far west as present-day Austria until they were forced back to Constantinople, which then became known as Istanbul.

The atrocities and massacres that took place during the Crusades were legendary and despite the argument that the actions were defensive, the aggressiveness of preemptive strikes and the brutality of the Crusaders certainly did not speak of the law of love that Christ taught.

The Hajj

A requirement of Islam is that devout Muslims, if at all possible, should make a pilgrimage to Mecca, the central location of Islam, at least once during their lifetime. It's one of the Five Pillars of Faith as described in the Quran and is noted to be the "farewell pilgrimage" of the Prophet Muhammad and his followers in 632 CE.

The Saudi government is the host for the hajj pilgrimage and it occurs annually according to the Islamic calendar. Pilgrimages are also possible at other times, but at other times, they are referred to as "the umrah". The hajj pilgrims arrive in the country at Jeddah before proceeding to Mecca. Each step is carefully controlled and orchestrated and pilgrims must be part of a group that is led by a guide. Men don special hajj uniforms that consist of two sheets of white fabric that symbolize purity and spirituality.

Women's clothing must be long, loose and cover their entire body and they must cover their hair completely with a hijab or headscarf. The hajj is for Muslims only, with approximately two million or more participants taking part each year.

The *Meqat* is the entire area in and around Mecca that includes all of the holy sites. As flights approach carrying Muslims for the hajj, an announcement is made so that passengers can make their intentions known (part of the ritual).

Men chant loudly, "Here I am, oh Lord, Here I am"; women also repeat this phrase but in a more subdued voice. Thereafter follows five days of visits to holy sites and the rites and rituals that accompany them.

The Ka'ba or the House of Allah is in the courtyard of the Grand Mosque or Sacred Mosque (Masjid al Haram) in Mecca. It is a house-size cube that has a portion of a black stone allegedly embedded into the eastern corner by Muhammad himself. The stone's original source is said to have fallen from heaven (a possible meteorite) as an indication for where Adam was to build an altar to God. The flood during the time of Noah destroyed the altar, but it was at this same place that Abraham's faith was also tested when God commanded him to sacrifice his son, Ishmael.

Later, Abraham and Ishmael returned to the desert and rebuilt the Ka'ba. By the time of Muhammad, it housed hundreds of pagan gods, which were destroyed by Muhammad himself leaving only Abraham's original monotheistic God/Allah.

As pilgrims enter the courtyard of the *Ka'bajmah*, they are dressed in white to perform what is known as the *tawaf*. The ritual begins at the black stone where pilgrims are encouraged to either kiss or touch the stone as they circumambulate the Ka'ba counter-clockwise seven times while chanting prayers and contemplating how one's life should revolve around Allah.

The Ka'ba, except for the door to the inside, is covered with a black silk cloth called the *kiswah*. The ritual of circumnavigation is carried out at the beginning of the hajj pilgrimage and again at the end.

The Grand Mosque and the surrounding area, including the courtyard, consists of eighty-eight acres and has been beautified and modernized by bin Laden Construction Company. It has a capacity for 733,000 pilgrims, has fifty-six escalators, and over a thousand places for ritual washing/purification before Islamic prayer.

Photography is not permitted in this area and both genders are permitted to walk this part of the hajj together. Women should expose their faces as Muhammad's wives did, but women *must* have a male chaperone per the Saudi government even though this requirement is not a directive from the Quran.

Very close to the Ka'ba, and now part of the Grand Mosque complex, is Safa and Marwa. The two hills are located where Hagar searched for water for her infant son Ishmael. It is said that she ran seven times between the two hills searching for water until a crying Ishmael himself kicked the sand and caused water to trickle out.

This became known as the spring of Zamzam from which pilgrims will drink during the hajj after walking seven times between the two hills. This trek has been modernized for the pilgrims and includes air-conditioned tiled walkways between the two hills. The spring of Zamzam has taps installed into the Grand Mosque itself as well as to the tent city where hajj pilgrims are housed three miles away in Mina.

The next important event is that of a visit to Mount Arafat, which occurs on the second day of the pilgrimage. Muhammad delivered his final sermon from this place after he completed his last hajj. It is a day for special prayers (Zuhr and Asr) and pilgrims spend the entire day until sundown on the mountain. It is a day of glorifying God, a day of supplication and repentance, judgment and forgiveness—a day of truth and liberation from sins. It is said that all prayers sincerely given at this place will be granted.

Pilgrims travel from there on to Muzdalifah near Mina where they will stay for three days sleeping outside or in tents. This ritual commemorates Abraham's temptation by the devil to disobey God when he was commanded by God to sacrifice his son Ishmael. The ritual consists of gathering small stones that are thrown at three pillars representing the devil's three attempts to dissuade Abraham from sacrificing Ishmael. Seven stones are thrown at each pillar for each of three days.

The pathway to this area was formerly notorious for its crowding and potential trampling by around two million pilgrims daily. The way was littered, hot, and difficult. It has since been modernized and includes train service to move pilgrims safely and more efficiently. Pilgrims must gather their own stones for throwing.

After this experience, like Abraham, whom Allah commanded to sacrifice a ram to spare Ishmael, Muslim pilgrims are expected to do the same after stoning the devil. Today, this can be accomplished by contacting a slaughterhouse near Mecca to make the sacrifice in their name with the pilgrims then receiving a text message to confirm their obligation has been fulfilled. Muslims can sacrifice a ram at any time, not only during the hajj, to give thanks for the good fortune and blessings they have received.

After the stoning ritual, known as the *Jamarat*, pilgrims return to Mecca to circle the Ka'ba once again. A throng of people at this last event has the potential to crush the hordes of pilgrims that finish this last circumnavigation of the Ka'ba. As the hajj is concluded, men have their heads shaved and women emulate this by cutting a lock of their hair.

Sharia Law

Until his death, Muhammad arbitrated justice regarding human disputes. He was the supreme judge for the community who resolved legal problems by interpreting, applying, and expanding the general provisions of the Quran and therefore God's commandments. *Sharia*, meaning path or way, is thought to be the revealed law of God that are commandments for Muslim society. Although the formative source for Sharia should remain unchanged, the laws society was meant to abide by should be reinterpreted according to the changing times.

Sharia not only defines relationships with one's neighbors and with the state, it also describes God's requirements of man such as rituals of daily prayer, giving to charity, fasting and a pilgrimage to Mecca. It is not only a system of law and justice but also a comprehensive code for public as well as private behavior.

After Muhammad's death, the divine revelations became fixed and immutable with "the way" much more static and inflexible than during Muhammad's life. Many thought that since Sharia law is divinely imposed, society, despite the changing circumstances that come with the passage of time should not be permitted to change.

Sharia law is derived from the following sources:

1.   The Quran, as revealed to Muslims through the angel Gabriel (Jibril).

2.   The actions and words of Muhammad (sunnah) preserved as the Hadith.

3.   Consensus of legal experts on any specific point of law (figh).

4.   Legal reasoning by analogy or previous decisions on similar cases.

The most-straight forward of these sources is the Quran. The sunnah or the actions and words of Muhammad, which were written down by the Hadith people, are also considered to be a key resource since they are based on eyewitness reports of Muhammad's actions and judgments and are thus considered appropriate to form the collection of maxims and practices as a reliable source for sharia law.

Jurists and religious scholars with special insights can be included if needed to resolve questions about the law. Their independent reasoning and legal opinions are called fatwas. On occasion, different interpretations of the law have emerged with sometimes separate and different treatments for the masses as opposed to the elite.

Religious scholars called ulama, and judges called qaids, are specially trained for the purpose of interpretation of the law. If a question or situation is addressed in the Quran, or by the divinely inspired traditions of the Prophet (the Sunnah), implementation of the law should follow those sources.

Many schools of law arose out of the differing social environments during the time when Islam was spread throughout different cultures and different geographical areas, and interpretations had a specific, local insight. To resolve disputes, precedents set by similar cases that had been resolved by the Quran or *Sunnah* were often used.

To add confusion, it has been alleged that some accounts attributed to the Sunnah and used for judgment were, in reality, the views of later jurists who falsely attributed their interpretation to that of the Prophet.

Religious scholars known as *muftis*, who are experts in Islamic law, have also interpreted sharia law. If there's a legal dispute regarding family or financial matters, it's handled in a *qadi* court by a judge (a *qadi*) who has legal training. In difficult cases, a qadi judge might ask a mufti for advice and a legal opinion. There are also *mazalim* courts, whose purpose is to "right wrongs" according to the spirit of sharia. These courts are somewhat loose but often are attended by qadis or muftis to ensure that the decisions do not conflict with Sharia law. Police, according to local customs, are sometimes only loosely associated with sharia and may themselves adjudicate less serious crimes.

There are two types of punishment contingent upon the category of crime. Crimes that are known as *hudud*, sometimes referred to as *hadd*, are those offenses particularly specified in the Quran or the Hadith. Punishments for those offenses are also described there.

Tazir punishments are at the discretion of a judge for crimes that are not mentioned in the Quran. Murder, bodily harm, and property damage, whether intentional or unintentional are civil or societal disputes and the victims or the victim's heirs are given options to either forgive the perpetrator or demand retribution and/or accept compensation.

Categories of traditional Sharia law are: Crimes against God or worship (Five Pillars of Islam) including actions specifically delineated in the Quran, Penal law involving human or social relations (crime and punishment), Transactional law (business dealings), Dietary law (halal), Family law (marriage, divorce, dominion), and Inheritance law.

Sharia court proceedings require evidence for conviction as well as two eyewitnesses to testify orally of their direct knowledge of a contention or accusation. Usually these will be two adult Muslim males of established integrity and character. Women are permitted to testify; however, two women are required in place of one male. There is no court hierarchy or system for appeal.

After the Ottoman Empire fell, many countries with a Muslim majority population adopted legal systems that are secular. However, there are still some who rule and adjudicate using Sharia rule: Iran, Afghanistan (under the Taliban), and Saudi Arabia maintain systems whose judges all follow traditional Sharia rules for societal living and dealing with crimes. The ultra-conservative offshoots of Islam also practice strict Sharia law in all aspects of living. Most modern Muslims don't agree with this approach.

Ultra Conservative/Radical Islam

The first three generations of Islam are referred to as the *salaf* and are said to be Islam in its purest, most pious form. In the 1700's, Mohammed Ibn Abd al-Wahhab founded the most conservative of the

Islamic sects—that of Wahhabism, which is alleged to be based on the salaf period. It is an offshoot of Sunni Islam and insists on a literal interpretation of the Quran with the assertion that only those who follow this path are "true believers, the chosen ones and the ones who will go to heaven."

According to Wahhabism, those who do not practice this form of Islam are not devout Muslims but are merely claimants of Islam. Wahhabists stress absolute sovereignty of Allah and the absence of any intercession by Muhammad, who is only a messenger. It denounces pilgrimages to tombs of saints or shrines by destroying them. Wahhabists enforce public attendance at prayer, forbid shaving for men, smoking of tobacco or the use of alcohol. Mosques must be unadorned and there are no representations of Muhammad or other living beings permitted.

Wahhabism, which began in one region of Saudi Arabia several centuries ago, was adopted and practiced by a member of the Saudi ruling class and has deeply influenced law. It is the rule of state in Saudi Arabia and is explicitly and openly opposed to Shia Islam. Because Saudi Arabia is the protector of Mecca and therefore the hajj pilgrimage, those who profess Islam without following the austere practices might be excommunicated while attending hajj.

Wahhabism has become increasingly influential recently because Saudi money from petroleum exports and charities has been a source of funding for Wahhabi *madrassas* (schools) and mosques in various places in the world. The goal is to expedite the replacement of liberal Sunni Islam with the more conservative Wahhabism. Although it has been the *official* declaration of the Saudi Grand Mufti, who issues legal edicts, fatwas and other jurisprudence interpretations, that "extremism, radicalism and terrorism do not belong to Islam in any way," it is alleged that Wahhabism, learned in the Saudi-funded madrassas, has spawned several terrorist organizations in spite of the fact that this was not their intent.

Al Qaeda

Al Qaeda, which means "the Base", is a group founded by Osama bin Laden that is violently opposed to the United States for its involvement in the Gulf War of 1991 and later in Somalia. Al Qaeda established and maintains cells in Sudan, Egypt, Saudi Arabia, Yemen, Somalia, Eritrea, Djibouti, Afghanistan, Pakistan, Bosnia, Croatia, Albania, Algeria, Tunisia, Lebanon, the Philippines, Tajikistan, Azerbaijan, Chechnya (Russia) and Kashmiri (India). It provides guesthouses and training camps and a stated intent to acquire nuclear weapons. Al Qaeda has issued fatwas against American troops in Saudi Arabia, Yemen and Somalia, all "nonbelievers", and generally against all American citizens.

African Groups

North Africa has several groups of extremists that may not have specifically arisen from Al Qaeda; however, most have some sort of formalized relationship with it.

Al-Shabaab's origin is in Somalia. The group uses social media to recruit Muslims from overseas and is a staunch provider of punishment based on their interpretation of Islamic law: stoning for adulterers, amputation of hands for thieves etc. It has banned music and showing videos of football matches. It carries out suicide attacks and is responsible for a shopping mall attack in Kenya that killed sixty-seven innocent people.

Boko Haram, which translates to "western education is forbidden", is a group operating mainly out of Nigeria. It targets police stations, churches, schools and other educational institutions. It is responsible for kidnapping 254 schoolgirls, many of whom were, after their capture, "married" to militants. Similar groups who are anti-American are found in Tunisia and Libya and are responsible for the incident at Benghazi.

The Taliban is thought by some to have emerged from religious seminaries and madrassas sponsored by Saudi Arabia in northern Pakistan after the withdrawal of Soviet troops from Afghanistan in 1990. After taking power in both Pakistan and Afghanistan, the Taliban were supposed to "restore" peace, provide security, and enforce Sharia law. The Taliban supports Islamic punishments for crimes and insists that women must wear burkas, despite the fact that this is not stated in the Quran.

The Taliban have banned television, music, cinema and education of girls over the age of ten, which resulted in the shooting of schoolgirl Malala Yousafzai on her way home from a Pakistani school. The Taliban also took responsibility for dynamiting two of the largest likenesses of the Buddha that were carved into a mountain in the Bamiyan valley in Afghanistan during the fourth and fifth centuries. They claimed the statues were idols and therefore violated the law. After September 2001, the Taliban were thought to have protected Osama bin Laden and the al-Qaeda movement.

ISIS

Finally, the Islamic State, (IS) was founded and led by Abu Musab al-Zarqawi who swore allegiance to Osama bin Laden when the U.S. invaded Iraq. It was initially known as al-Qaeda of Iraq (AQI). The group became a major force of insurgency. After Zarqawi's death, IS evolved into the Islamic State of Iraq (ISI) and Abu Bakr al-Baghdadi, a former U.S. detainee, became the new leader by overtaking large areas in Syria and Iraq after the U.S. pulled all its troops out of the country.

The group then declared itself an Islamic state ("Islamic State in Iraq and Syria" ISIS) and professed it was a "caliphate" (Allah's deputy) that would reinstate Islamic Sharia law. It has demanded all Muslims everywhere in the world swear allegiance to this cause. The goal of ISIS is to eradicate obstacles and to restore Allah's rule on earth as well as to protect itself from infidels. The brutality of ISIS is infamous and includes, suicide bombers, mass killing and abductions for ransom, beheadings, brutal attacks, and killings in several European countries. It has recruited members through social media and has seized military equipment from Iraq left by the U.S. including heavy weapons, surface-to-air missiles, rocket launchers etc.

ISIS welcomes the prospect of a direct confrontation with the West likening it to the showdown between Muslims and their enemies as described by apocalyptic prophecies. ISIS has raised millions of dollars for this cause from stolen oil and refinery products as well as ransom payments from kidnappings, extortion, selling antiquities, and selling girls and women as sex slaves.

An eerie, but somewhat unsubstantiated warning recorded in the Hadith (the Prophet's actions and sayings), states: "If you see the black flags, then hold your ground and do not move your hands or your feet. A people will come forth who are weak and have no capability, their hearts are like blocks of iron. They are the people of the State, they do not keep a promise or a treaty.

They call to the truth but they are not its people. Their names are nicknames and their last names are the names of towns and cities, like Al Halabi or al-Baghdadi and their hair is loose like women's hair. Leave them until they fight among themselves, then Allah will bring the truth from whoever He wills".

References/Bibliography

Arberry, A.J. (1955). *The Koran interpreted*. New York: Macmillan.

Dawood. N. J. (1956). *The Koran*. New York: Penguin Books.

Pickthall, M. M. *The meaning of the glorious Koran*. New York: Mentor Books. (Twelfth Printing).

Ali, A. Y. (2010 Edition). *The Qur'an: A guide and mercy*. New York: Tahrike Tarsile Qur'an, Inc.

Armstrong, K. (2000). *Islam: A short history*. New York: Modern Library Chronicles.

Armstrong, K. (1992). *Muhammad: A biography of the Prophet*. New York: Harper Collins.

Armstrong, K. (1996). *Jerusalem: One city, three faiths*. New York: Ballantine Books.

Coulson, N.J. (2017). "Shariah: Islamic law." Encyclopaeida Britannica. Retrieved September 17, 2017, from http://www.britannica.com/topic/Shariah.

Doyne, S. (2016). "What Muslims do on hajj, and why." Retrieved on September 15, 2016, from http://learning.blogs.nytimes.com/2016/09/12/article-of-the-day-what-muslims-do-on-hajj-and-why.

Haley, A. (2015). *Malcolm X*. New York: Ballantine Books.

Hazelton, L. (2009). *After the Prophet: The epic story of the Shia-Sunni split*. New York: Anchor Books.

Helminski, K. & Henzell-Thomas, J. (2008). *The book of Hadith: Sayings of the Prophet Muhammad from the Mishkaat al-Masabih*. Watsonville, CA: The Book Foundation.

Husayn, S. & Ja'fari, M. (2014). *The origins and early development of Shia Islam*. New York: Talee.

Mashal, Mujib & Sukhanyar, Jawad. (2017). *Taliban target: Scholars of Islam,* Retrieved September 17, 2017, from http://nytimes.com/.../uptick-in-killing.

McLean, W. (2017). "Dome of the Rock." Encyclopedia Britannica online. Retrieved September 17, 2017, from http://britannica.com/topic/Dome-of-the-Rock>.

Nasr, V. (2007). *The Shia revival: How conflicts with Islam will shape the future.* New York: W.W. Norton & Company.

Nomani, A. Q. (2005). *Standing alone: An American woman's struggle for the soul of Islam.* New York: Harper Collins.

Reporter. (2017). "What is Wahhabism? The reactionary branch of Islam from Saudi Arabia said to be 'the main source of global terrorism". The Telegraph online. Retrieved on September 17, 2017, from http://www.telegraph.co.uk/.

Reporter. (2013). "Africa's militant Islamist groups." BBC online. Retrieved on September 17, 2017, from http:// www.BBC.com.

Reporter. (2015). "What is 'Islamic State'?" BBC online. Retrieved on September 17, 2017, from http://www.BBC.com.

Reporter. (2016). "Who are the Taliban?" BBC online. Retrieved on September 17, 2017, from http://www.BBC.com.

Reporter. (2015). "Background: Al Qaeda." NPR online. Retrieved on September 17, 2017, from http://www.npr.org.

Smith, H. (1991). *The World's Religions.* New York: HarperCollins.

Tarsa, A. (2015). *Being Muslim: A practical guide.* U.S.: Sandala Inc.

ॐ

HINDUISM

Several thousand years before the birth of Jesus and hundreds of years before God spoke with Abraham, a diverse group of people known as Aryans lived in the Indus river valley, and together with the existing cultures, became the land called Bharat, which is Sanskrit for "land of the rising sun of full knowledge". These inhabitants became the predecessors of modern-day India.

Originally, by custom, the people were divided by mental inclinations into four distinct classes: the *brahmins*, who were the priests, the *ksatriya* who were the warriors, the *vaisaya* who were the farmers, and the *sudras* who became the outcastes.

This social order remained until the twentieth century. The brahmins (Aryan meaning "noble") were learned and became the spiritual leaders who performed rituals and rites of worship to the Supreme God that united all living things. They were the practitioners for the Vedic religion in India and their primary duty was to preserve, protect and propagate the ancient rituals and to lead hymns and poetic verses in the ancient language of Sanskrit. Their obligation was to serve the populace and act as intermediaries to connect them to the Supreme God.

The Vedic Sanskrit rites are described in the first portion of the scriptures known as the Vedas, which means "revealed knowledge". The end section of the Vedas is the experiential knowledge known as the Upanishads. This philosophy is known as Vedanta. It is the Vedas plus spiritual knowledge or wisdom and was given to humanity at the beginning of time by the Supreme God. It has relevance for everyone as the eternal path of spiritual realization that answers all questions of life and shows the way beyond sorrow. There are four separate collections: The Rig Veda, Sama Veda, Yajur Veda, and Atharva Veda and included with each are their rites and hymns.

Eventually, a time came when truth seekers desired a more direct connection with the Supreme God, and they began to question spiritual matters and to experiment in order to establish a more intimate, personal relationship with the Supreme. Writings of the learned wisdom that was gained by trial and error and experimentation were recorded by many of the illuminated sages, *rishis-gurus*, who, in turn, took on aspiring apprentices who desired spiritual instruction.

These master teachers were the removers of ignorance or darkness. They taught and discussed with their spiritual seekers such questions as: What is the meaning of life? What is death? Why are humans born and reincarnated? What is the nature of God?

The written recordings of these *shruti* (discussions) between teacher and aspirant became known as the Upanishads. The Upanishads, in turn, developed into the core of the religion later known as Hindu and they became an experiential guide to discover one's Self: *Santana Dharma* or universal and Eternal Tradition of Truth for all time. It wasn't until the 15th century that the Santana Dharma became known as the Hindu religion.

Santana Dharma is meant for all beings and for the whole of the universe. It is based on self-realization and the search for the eternal truth of the meaning of life, death, and life's purpose. It is open to all approaches rather than through a certain personality, a book, an institution or an organization and it recognizes the unity of all human beings despite different beliefs and cultures. It consists of universal truths considered eternal and for all people with the ultimate goal of oneness with the Divine. It also recognizes the process of evolution and its impact on both religion and on human consciousness, which require relevancy to current times.

Although there were *many* Upanishads, ten or twelve major ones have been studied extensively. The Upanishads recorded the internal experience of consciousness, the connection with God, and the realization that all of humanity—you and I, him and her are one with God of the universe. You are That!

A teacher or guru is recommended to guide and interpret the recorded knowledge of the Upanishads for the aspirant and to enable the realization of how to liberate oneself from endless cycles of reincarnation—birth and death—*samsara*.

Creation

From ancient times to the present day, several schools of Hindu philosophy have evolved, and this accounts for the several theories of creation. The Vedantic philosophy (derived from the Vedas) considers creation to be a beginning and endless infinite series of cycles of creations and dissolutions. The physical world is manifested from God and then unmanifested as it returns to the creator to then again begin anew.

Each cycle, from the beginning of one creation to the beginning of another creation or re-creation is termed a *"kalpa"*, which means "eon" in Sanskrit. A kalpa consists of 4.32 billion years as it is counted in the current age of our planetary system.

With each new creation, two types of resident reality evolve: that of pure consciousness or spirit, and that of unconscious primordial matter. Both are uncaused but exist. From the pure primordial matter evolves the universe as the matter gradually changes and transforms into a world of physicality, as we know it. From this matter, elements of earth, air, fire and space are generated from subtle to gross. Pure consciousness, on the other hand, forms ego, intellect, mind and sense organs and through various combinations, different species are created including their individual identities and consciousness within each physical being.

Karma and Reincarnation

Segments of the Upanishad texts, as recorded by the sages, discuss the law of cause and effect known as *karma*. Humans are created and embodied with a free-will consciousness, a personality, and identity (ego), and a deeper, inner consciousness (the True Self) known as *Atman*, or that which is a part of the Supreme God, *Brahman*.

Physical life experiences are granted for the purpose of fulfilling worldly cravings, which may be sensual in nature or perhaps that of gaining wealth or power. Or, they may be spiritual desires in service to God. The things one desires trigger free-will actions to attain them. In their fulfillment, an individual may achieve them with positive actions, or the manner of acquisition may be negative in nature. This means the things we want may be accomplished with utmost righteousness and integrity or, on the contrary, achieved by unscrupulous conduct with a negative result for someone or something.

Each and every action of an individual, even one's thoughts, must be accounted for as one lives and interacts with other beings day by day. Actions that exploit another or cause harm result in a negative karma while actions of merit reap benefits or lessen a previous negative karmic debt, which must sooner or later be paid.

Reincarnation occurs life cycle after life cycle (known in Sanskrit as *samsara*), until a being has satisfied all their wants and cravings and has reconciled the bad karma—the hurt or harm they have caused others. One's destiny is to ultimately evolve spiritually until it is realized that only the bliss and peace of being one with the Supreme God is the real desire. The achievement of oneness is *nirvana* and when this is attained, samsara is ended, and reincarnation is no longer necessary.

Until nirvana is achieved and there is no further need for physical life, it is the Hindu belief that the body, which is an impermanent, finite manifestation of an individual, is shed as one might discard an overcoat. Even though one's life ends, and the body is discarded, One's consciousness, including the Atman remains and is reincarnated into another body. Likewise, accumulated karma, one's merits or negative action's accounting, is also carried over. For this reason, karma may endure for many lifetimes until it is eventually reconciled.

God is considered neutral and is not responsible for the pleasure or pain or the punishment and rewards individuals experience. Rather, the responsibility is that of the individual who makes free-will choices. God is the observer of the law of truth, but not the administrator of justice. Samsara or rebirth cycles allow for the repayment of negative karma or with positive karma, one may reap benefits with a rebirth.

To further understand how karma operates, it can be demonstrated in two ways. Actions of this lifetime that have an immediate effect, such as a heinous crime—murder for example—normally have a reaction and punishment within the same lifetime. This is called *kriyamana or agami* karma.

Other good or bad actions that are relatively trivial compared to that of heinous crimes, accumulate. This is known as *sanchita karma*. Along with actions that may produce effects later on, these karmic debts and rewards are reconciled in the future—often in a future lifetime.

As karma is accumulated a kinetic-like force builds up and must be addressed. An individual with the accumulation of karmic debt will be born into a circumstance befitting the debt, which can explain the inequity of one's birth. It's a Hindu belief that living in a sub-human state for several lifetimes in order to pay off a very bad karma or conversely, living on a higher enlightened plane, such as a god or goddess or an angel, to reap the benefit of good actions, can occur. Envision a spiritual ledger book of plusses and minuses.

With the exception of grace, which may be bestowed on those who perform good deeds for God alone without the expectation of receiving anything in return, reincarnation is the only opportunity to resolve one's accumulated karma and to achieve spiritual progress. The only other possibility is that on occasion, there is an incarnation of an avatar of the Supreme God, who may occupy a physical body created for the purpose of absolving negative karma. The Divine occupies this physical body in order to have a corporal presence in the physical world. With exceptional compassion, sins and bad karma that are present are absorbed into this earthly body, which will undergo extreme suffering to give relief and salvation to mankind from the large burden of accumulated negative karma.

It may be the case, that during an individual's earthly life, they may also want to pursue a life of perfection or one that is in concert with the goal to evolve spiritually. Even though most beings typically begin their physical existence seeking pleasure, then wealth, then success, and finally power as a means of fulfillment, Hinduism sees nothing wrong with pursuing these things even considering them to be part of a soul's journey that may continue for many lifetimes. At some point however, mundane desires become saturated and less meaningful, in which case an individual will want a more significant and satisfying goal. A realization occurs that the self-centeredness of one's previous hankerings has little meaning and eventually the quest for deeper significance takes over. A sense of duty and harmony with community may become the goal with a concurrent wish for the betterment and evolution of humanity.

At last, something beyond the earthly or physical plane inspires an individual to probe beyond the finiteness of the everyday world with its recurring cycles of birth and death. Rather than seeking earthly pleasures, the desire now becomes that of liberation from the finite to the infinite and eternal satisfaction. This quest may frequently occur at a stage in life when other duties are no longer pressing i.e. the family has been raised to adulthood and one is free of distractions and self-serving interests. With time available to pursue a more meditative focus on the truest meaning beyond the confines of earthly interests, an aspirant may leave society behind to follow a path of solitude and meditation in search of the Absolute God and a search for eternal fulfillment. Several paths are available to achieve this based on one's inclination such as life in solitude as a forest dweller away from civilization, or life in an ashram where others of like-mind abide.

Spiritual Paths and Their Practices

An individual can choose two different spiritual paths: one is that of a householder, as mentioned above, and is referred to as *Pravritti Marga*; the other is *Nivritti Marga* or renunciation. The path of Pravritti Marga is when a person raises a family and lives a life in which there are sensual earthly desires. Eventually, however, the one underlying goal to realize God becomes the foremost desire. In selecting this path in life, a person's behavior should be thought of as a service to God, and in so doing, have concern for all beings including the poor and homeless. There should be engagement in honest work to provide for the family, making certain they are cared for with the necessities to live comfortably. There should be deep respect and gratitude toward one's parents, looking on them as representing God. One's spouse should be precious and cared for tenderly and generously without desiring another, even in thought.

One should not brag or break confidences that have been given to him or her by others. Material things should not be overly attended to and one should maintain cleanliness of body as well as purity of heart. Men should demonstrate bravery and resist evil with force if necessary; yet they should be gentle with friends and relatives. For one's children, they should be educated and when they are grown, treated as equals. If a brother or sister is in need or their children are wanting, they should be cared for. Likewise, the poor and needy should be remembered and cared for and there should be deep respect for others who are good and honest.

Only people who have noble qualities should be befriended. One should maintain a good name and speak the truth at all times and not harm (*ahimsa*) or cause trouble for others. One should not be lazy or idle and if wealth is achieved, it should be used to help others. One should participate in social service for the betterment of the community.

For the path of Nivritti Marga, there is a renunciation of sensual desires and the aspirant dedicates his life to achieving the goal of realization of God. As a monk, one is celibate; his life is simple, as he owns nothing. He will beg for food to sustain himself and it is householders' duty to feed and care for the 'renunciate'. He has no home but lives in a cave, a temple, a hut, or even under a tree. He is truthful, nonviolent, serene and compassionate and his behavior to all he encounters is kind. He spends his life studying the scriptures and meditating to find God.

Pathways to God: Yoga

To reach God, there are four major pathways: *Bhakti Yoga, Jnana Yoga, Raja Yoga, Karma Yoga.* Yoga is the connecting link for communion with God and each of these yoga practices appeal to persons who have different personality traits. All paths to the infinite God contain meditative, mental work and the guidance of a spiritual teacher.

For Bhakti Yoga, a path of love and devotion, the emotion of love—the highest form of expression—is directed to God by different attitudes such as a serene servant of God, as one's dearest friend, as a mother loves her child, the love of a wife for her husband (not sensual however) or perhaps from the perspective of God as the Divine Mother. From one of these viewpoints and with meditative worship, the love developed by an aspirant becomes more and more intense until God is realized.

In Jnana Yoga, the aspirant has a rational attitude with a method of concentration so that the divine Self, the Atman, is discovered, which is ultimately the same as the Divine Supreme God in all. It is a process of elimination method as the devotee is initially a doubter and must eventually eliminate the physical, the senses, the ego or "I"-ness and everything that is not the real inner Self. When the focus finally shifts to the inner being and the "Self" aspect is recognized and cannot be negated, the physical concerns disappear, and Truth is experienced. It is here that the oneness of Atman (Self) with Brahman (the Supreme God) is realized.

Raja Yoga, founded by Patanjali, is for the curious and natural explorer and the goal is to know one's own mind as the means of discovery. This method has eight progressive steps: 1) abstinence from falsehoods, carnal desires and passions including no harm to others; 2) cultivation of good habits of body and mind, austerity and study of spiritual things; 3) sitting postures for prolonged meditation; 4) breath control to calm the mind for optimal concentration; 5) withdrawal from senses and external objects; 6) fixing the mind on an object of contemplation; 7) contemplation for long time periods with greater intensity, yet with distinction of the object and the meditator; and finally 8) the most intense concentration on an object until the mind actually becomes a part of the object upon which it is meditating. The "I" disappears, and the aspirant is no longer an independent being but merged into the object of concentration.

The mind with its accumulation of all previous thoughts buried in the subconscious becomes purified during this process and harmful impressions are released and dispersed allowing the divine Self to become illuminated and to shine through. The pure light of the Self can then merge with the Divine. This is the goal for the devotee in Raja Yoga.

The individual must be chaste in thought, word, and deed with a purified mind. One should be guided by an experienced teacher for this method to avoid mishaps that are said to possibly cause mental problems and even insanity. In the course of Raja Yoga practice, it is said that extraordinary powers can be achieved that are supernatural—such as entering another's body, making oneself invisible, possessing knowledge of the future, the ability to fly, understanding the language of animals and other feats that are incomprehensible and unattainable for normal humans. The devotee should not be tempted to use any of these powers but should ignore them and move through the process and progress to the inherent divinity within. This is the real goal.

Raja Yoga uses dormant spiritual energy within an aspirant that lies at the base of the spine, called *kundalini*. Through the intensity of the meditation, this energy "awakens" and begins moving upward toward the individual's brain. It passes through seven centers or levels called *chakras* where a new and different spiritual experience occurs. When the kundalini power reaches the uppermost chakra in the brain, the individual becomes spiritually illuminated.

Lastly, there is the path of Karma Yoga—that of right action. The aspirant does not withdraw from the world but works to help others by doing good. The caveat here is that one does good without attachment to the outcome, i.e. there is no expectation that there will be a profit or benefit for the doer other than to help others. The object of this work is service to God. Its motive is unselfish with the intent to ultimately purify the doer and to know God in all beings. Having acknowledged this exception, the actions are primarily for the sake of God rather than for the benefit of the doer.

God and Worship

God is beyond comprehension and unknowable by ordinary human minds. Beyond space, time and cause, God is transcendent, eternal and changeless—so believed the sages of the Indo-Aryan forefathers. This God is the creator of the universe and is ruler over all peoples. This Supreme One became known as Brahman—Eternal Existence, Absolute Knowledge and Infinite Bliss.

When one tries to imagine the infinite Brahman with man's finite mind, the result is most likely a finite image with characteristics that have human meaning. Because of this, Brahman is often given human traits that give relevance to humans. This humanized God is known as Ishvara and from this form (that gives meaning to the lower human mind) further separation into other meaningful images may occur depending upon the needs of the devotee. For example, Ishvara may take on different presentation characteristics depending upon the role it takes. When Ishvara creates, he is "Brahma"; when he preserves, he is "Vishnu"; when he destroys, he is "Shiva". Although the pronoun "he" has been used, the manifestations of the Supreme One (God) are genderless. The different appearances are for no other purpose than to establish connections that provide meaning to humans. The manifestations and the relationships they provide enable a closer relationship with God for those who require substantive images.

Hinduism recognizes the meritorious work of humanity. Although a human soul may not yet be liberated from the burden of karma and thus incurs recurring reincarnations, at the end of his/her virtuous earthly life, an individual may be rewarded with deification to that of a Deva (masculine) or Devi (feminine). The Sanskrit word "div" means "to shine"; however, with karmic deification, when the accumulated good karma runs out, the deity will once again become an ordinary human.

The first Deva, Hiranyagarbha, is a creation of Ishvara who became a sort of permanent overseer for other deities that have followed. By the will of Ishvara, who we have said is a manifested form of Brahman, the Devas and Devis possess divine powers that may be further extended to human devotees.

For this reason, Hindi worshipers may direct their prayers toward a specific deity who has been granted special powers by Brahman to provide for specific needs. For example, *Sarasvati* is the personification of qualities of Ishvara and is the giver of knowledge and learning; *Lakshimi* personifies the virtues that are possible from wealth and prosperity; *Genesh* is a deva of beginnings and good fortunes and a remover of obstacles as well as a god leader of warriors, and Indra renders control over the arms and hands of all people. It should be clearly understood that Deva(i)s are not separate and different gods, they are merely separate and different manifestations that represent the qualities of the one God, Ishvara, who in turn is a personification of the Supreme God, Brahman. All have been given traits and characteristics that have meaning and significance for human understanding.

Mahabarata and the Bagavad Gita

The Mahabarata is the longest epic poem ever written. It is a poetic history of mankind written by Vyasa, a Vedic guru and sage. *Genesh*, the elephant-headed god of wisdom, beginnings, good fortunes, remover of obstacles, and leader of warriors, originally transcribed the text into ancient Sanskrit. *Genesh* is also a good listener—hence his large ears.

The poem records the acts of five sons, who are descendants of God in human form, and the ensuing chaos that evolves over time as the minds of men separate from their soul and the Supreme. It's a chronicle similar to that of Adam and Eve and their descendants. In the Mahabarata, two families find themselves in a situation of war over who should rule their kingdom, which was usurped by one family from those who should rightfully govern it.

The Bhagavad Gita is a portion of this poetic record that describes this occasion of war, which is, in truth, an allegory for the battle between good and evil. Hindus universally know the Bhagavat Gita portion of the Mahabarata as their primary life guide. It has also been called the Eastern equivalent to the Sermon on the Mount. It is important as it provides instructions and lessons on how to live and conduct one's life.

It has been said that Mahatma Ghandhi modeled his life from the Bagavad Gita. Its meaning provides a lesson that illustrates selfless action, void of selfish motives. This single section of literature has been translated into every major language and is timeless in its message. It is as relevant today as it was when first written thousands of years ago.

Arjuna, a warrior who is about to go to war, struggles with what will be the loss of lives in order to take back the kingdom that rightfully belongs to his clan from others who are of his more distant family. He is torn over the pending battle and has feelings of guilt because it is not a foreign enemy, but his own extended family.

Krisha is Arjuna's chosen charioteer; but in reality, Lord Krisha is an avatar of God, who acts as his spiritual advisor to reclaim what is rightfully his. He (Lord Krisha) is depicted in paintings with blue skin like a vast and infinite sky in order to be recognized as actually being the embodiment and incarnation of God. He represents the Atman deep within us—that which desires to be reunited with the supreme God (Brahman) but must deal with the "battles" of the human physical existence.

He is that small subtle voice—one's internal divine conscience— that is ever-present but not always recognized and acknowledged. Although the poem speaks of a war on the battlefield, in reality it represents the conflicts that are fought within the hearts of humans between good and evil, right and wrong, light and dark forces. Lord Krisha encourages Arjuna to do what he must do (go to battle without regard to any personal gain) for the reason that it is the just thing to do. If one's conscience is followed, one should have the self-mastery to conquer what truly is one's heritage, a victorious life and the realization of God.

Rama and Sita

All in India know this famous story. It has been written as a fairy tale for children and has many versions, yet the same message. It has been told and retold, acted out with puppets, and written for children's books in many languages. Its moral follows the theme of the Bhagavat Gita in that it focuses on the overcoming of evil with good.

Where the Bhagavat Gita is an allegory of the internal war within an individual between good and evil, the tale of Rama and Sita tells of the capture of Sita, the wife of Rama, who is really Vishnu and an incarnation of the Divine. The story of Rama and Sita, is a tale that portrays evil demons as well as animal and human heroes.

Philosophically, the animals in the story represent our lower nature and instincts. Lord Rama guides them all to salvation, and together, the Good rescue Sita from the evil forces that have captured her and goodness overcomes evil. This story is the basis for India's Dewali celebration when every house, regardless of how poor its inhabitants are, places a light in the window to symbolize good over evil, light over darkness.

Upanishad Scriptures

To this day, study of the over a hundred Upanishads, which were originally written in Sanskrit as early as 4000 BCE, continues. The word Upanishad translates to "to sit near at the feet of the master". With the proper guidance, the correct understanding of the text is achieved. One may study for a lifetime—from youth to old age to discover life's purpose and to realize the Truth.

In the Bagavad Gita, the most renowned writing sums up the whole of the Upanishads and, as mentioned earlier, was a favorite of Mahatma Ghandhi. His study and practice of the Bagavad Gita teachings provided a model for how he lived his life and in particular his leadership and directives of peaceful descent that eventually gave India its freedom from British colonialism. Liberation of spirit liberates all humanity.

Of the Upanishads that still exist, and many have been lost, ten to twelve are considered to be the principal ones now taught to those seeking liberation. There were many that explored the mind and its inner realms and focused on the human experience of inner consciousness. Outwardly, this consciousness is manifested as intellect, love, action and experience (experience, for the most part, occurring through one's senses). But consciousness can also be directed inward through meditation in order to know the mind and the inner reality that unites all beings.

Through meditative practice, as one becomes and remains focused, it is possible to reach a state so steady and unwavering that the meditator may ultimately be absorbed into the object of contemplation and achieve insight into the inner mind. This insight, devoid of the senses, yields comprehension of the inner human experience including that, which unifies mankind. The sages who recorded the Upanishads attained the realization that consciousness exists in layers ranging from consciousness affected by the senses, to states of consciousness, or unconsciousness, during dreams and dreamless sleep. It's in dreamless sleep that the observing self can detach from the physical body and mind and find rest. This stillness of consciousness in the depths of the mind is always available and is where the real Self exists separate from body, mind, and senses. In this place is a world without the limitations of time, space or harm. It's where the underlying Realty of life is inherent, which is the essence of every created thing. It is this real Self that is one with the ultimate power that created and sustains the universe. It's in this place where one may discover who they really are, what their actual innate desires are, as well as develop an eventual resolve that will lead to fruition in a process called self-realization—that of knowing and becoming One with God.

To discover and know Brahman, the seeker must engage in deep concentration so that one may delve beyond the superficial thoughts of the sense-oriented mind. This is accomplished by meditation and a system of yoga. *Yoga*, literally translated means, "yoking" with the intent of "yoking" to God spiritually. Although in the west the term "yoga" implies a type of physical exercise, in India's spiritual quest, its meaning is to connect both the physical and mental individual to God—to yoke the inner Self with that of God—Atman with Brahman.

Eventually, one realizes that the body is one of many layers; a jacket or covering that surrounds the human personality and the inner true Self. Even the thing we call "the mind"—the senses, emotions, the intellect—are separate entities from the Reality that is the Self. When the processes of the mind are left behind and cease, one experiences peace at the threshold of pure being even though the one who experiences it may still have a personal identity.

From this state, the next phase is that of the disappearance of individuality when the Self "dissolves" into pure awareness—that of liberation and release—a oneness with Brahman, the ultimate Reality and that which is the essence of every living thing. This unification is pure, and the separateness of Self is eliminated and the Reality of Brahman is realized. It is a state of joy so sublime that all desires are fulfilled—for this state, is in actuality, one's only real desire.

This is the joy of the infinite, the native state from which we were once separated by our birth. As one leaves this state and reverts again into the processes of the mind, awareness of the physical and the personality resume. Having experienced this union with the Supreme, nothing finite will ever satisfy again except for this condition of absolute, pure awareness and unrestricted joy. To achieve this union permanently becomes our life's only true desire and our chosen destiny.

Individual Upanishad Summaries

Adi Shankara, a philosopher and theologian of the eighth century, became committed to rescue the Upanishads from centuries of neglect. Using the Upanishads as resources, the philosophical system and renaissance of sorts (Vedanta) emerged. The message is: "That which, by being known, everything else becomes known."

His writings emphasize that whatever we have done, whoever we are, in each of us resides an inalienable Self that is divine and transcends all else. We are reminded that that same bit of Self (Atman) dwells in all creatures and ultimately only love and compassion should be the objective for living in both the physical and the spiritual realm beyond death. Nothing is "other" from us as all creatures are one with God.

It goes without saying that an individual does not easily realize or attain this desired supreme state of liberation from human existence.

For this reason, the experiences of heaven and earthly existence provide transitory opportunities through reincarnation when the Self can learn from past mistakes and evolve toward the ultimate goal of liberation and become one with God. It's in this state of being one with God, that birth and death become meaningless and finally are no more.

The following excerpts from several Upanishads give examples and serve to describe these concepts:

> "When all desires that surge in the heart
> Are renounced, the mortal becomes immortal.
> When all the knots that strangle the heart
> Are loosened, the mortal becomes immortal.
> This sums up the teaching of the scriptures."
> (Katha II. 3. 14-15.)

All desires are satisfied or found insignificant. All bad deeds (that strangle the heart) are purified (through karma).

> "As a caterpillar, having come to the end of one
> Blade of grass, draws itself together and
> Reaches out for the next, so the Self,
> Having come to the end of one life and
> Shed all ignorance, gathers in its faculties and
> Reaches out from the old body to a new.
> (Brihadaranyaka III, 4.3.)

The continuity of a personality is not broken, but reincarnation allows the payment of karmic debt and evolution of the Self.

"The world is the wheel of God, turning round
And round with all living creatures upon its rim.
The world is the river of God,
Flowing from him and flowing back to him.
On this ever-revolving wheel of being
The individual self goes round and round
Through life after life, believing itself
To be a separate creature, until
It sees its identity with the Lord of Love
And attains immortality in the indivisible whole."
(Shvetashvatara I, 4-6.)

All creatures endure life and death as separate beings until there is the realization that all are one with the Lord of Love. Love unites all in the attainment of immortality. Then:

"As a lump of salt thrown in water dissolves
And cannot be taken out again, though
Wherever we taste the water it is salty, even
So, beloved, the separate self dissolves in the
Sea of pure consciousness, infinite and immortal.
Separateness arises from identifying the Self with
The body, which is made up of the elements; when
This physical identification dissolves, there can be
No more separate self. This is what I want to tell you."
(Brihadaranyaka II, 4.12.)

It is believed the Upanishads were written down by sages who considered them to be sacred inspirations for mankind. They recorded the experiences of men and women who achieved the understanding of the transcendent reality of God and the pathway one must take to be liberated from meaningless physical desires and to ultimately unite with God as one's only actual desire.

These writings, for the most part, emerged or originated in the Aryan-Indo era. They were teachings meant to be universal and a gift for all of humanity rather than for the creation of a specific religion.

The Hindu religion, nevertheless, was eventually established on these foundations even though, as with all concepts that have passed through time, there were points of disagreement and misunderstanding. Sri Ramakrishna, a nineteenth century Hindu mystic, suggested there are many paths leading to the same goal—that of knowing God. Furthermore, all paths are equal when their intent is to lead to God.

Hinduism: The Practice Today

Today Hinduism is the third largest world religion behind Christianity and Islam. It claims to be the oldest religion with roots that are traceable to the dawn of history. It is empirical in nature in that it is defined by inner practices of yoga and meditation rather than an outward identity with a defined system of beliefs. It is pluralistic in that it accepts that there are many pathways to God and Truth. Hinduism refers to its philosophy as Santana Dharma or the Eternal Tradition of Truth.

Dharma, defined as the laws of nature that apply to all beings, includes the laws of karma whereby good actions elevate the soul while harmful actions reduce it. Where most theological systems divide humanity into believers and non-believers according to their particular dogma, which may in turn be equated with good and evil, holy or unholy, the Santana Dharma argues that actions, good or bad, override any theology and religious beliefs.

The system of karma and reincarnation allows an individual to repay destructive actions with as many lifetimes as necessary to settle a negative score so that when this is achieved, the eventual solitary goal of self-knowledge can be accomplished. To seek out our true nature, our true purpose, and to discover the universal truth that applies to all beings, is the soul's highest desire. This leads to the final objective to become one with the Absolute, the Supreme, and to obtain enlightened consciousness beyond time and space.

Thus, there is unity of all despite religious differences, and there is a common desire and destiny for all souls. In Hinduism this may be accomplished with the practice of methods of asana, pranayama, mantra and meditation. Rather than being a belief-oriented practice with a written doctrine and code, the objectives of Hinduism are experiential.

The sense of unity that is sought is inclusive rather than exclusive and its philosophy respects all approaches to inner Truth. Hinduism values diversity and therefore does not seek converts. There is no prophet, no holy book, canon or dogma, no prescribed ritual, or particular day of worship. Its purpose is to guide an individual, through meditation, toward self-realization and the pursuit of Truth. It honors the Divine in others, but never imposes its beliefs or opinions on others. Yet, it is open to all who wish to be guided by its constructs.

Hinduism recognizes the Divine by many names and forms and from this multiplicity evolves its unity—different manifestations of the One or a unity that includes diversities of practices. Hinduism is progressive. It does not conflict with science, but accepts evolution, the notion of levels of consciousness, and the antiquity of the universe with its many repetitive cycles of creation and destruction.

Although it consists of a complete system of sacred and spiritual arts, it also incorporates all sciences including medicine, astrology, architecture, music, dance, literature, yogic, and occult. It is based in Sanskrit and includes comprehensive rituals as well as Divine incarnations via avatars, gurus, rishis, yogis, sages, and seers who act as guides for individuals who wish to obtain self-knowledge. However, these guides are not recognized as prophets or saviors.

Sanatana Dharma espouses that there is One Truth that is eternal and unchanging and it is not dependent upon any specific dogma or authoritative system of beliefs. It declares that the ultimate destiny of all individuals is to aspire to and search for a higher awareness of universal principles by the elimination of ignorance.

It does not recognize sin as such but maintains ignorance is the cause of wrong action. With a thorough understanding of the natural laws (dharma), one will discover the unity and interdependence of nature and of all beings. With this understanding of the underlying universal Truth, separateness and conflict dissolve. As with physical laws such as gravity that operate for all beings, so too, the same spiritual laws are constant and apply to everyone.

> "As rivers flowing to the sea discard their names and forms, so the person of spiritual knowledge, liberated from name and form enters into that celestial Being that transcends all."
> (Mundaka Upanishad III.2.8.)

According to the Santana Dharma, an important tenet for all religious beliefs, including Hinduism, is that they should be questioned, and doubts examined and verified. Furthermore, there is no one group or organization that owns Truth to be dispensed as an exclusive belief. Because the Divine dwells in all beings, all beings should be honored and valued for their divineness. Truth is therefore ONE and universal—NOT exclusive to one group, but inclusive of all. One's good or bad actions determine the debt that is required for retribution. Kindness, compassion and charitable living equilibrate and cancel past debts thereby enabling one to seek unity and enlightenment.

Common Hindu values and attitudes that can be shared by all faiths are the hallmark of the realization that all beings are connected. By hurting others, Self is damaged. Non-violence, truthfulness, self-discipline, compassion, loving kindness, charity, and service to others are important behaviors that acknowledge and recognize the unity of all beings. These characteristics are inclusive of all faiths.

Finding the Truth is an individual endeavor and it cannot be accomplished by merely being a member of a group or association. It is the ultimate goal and destiny of one's individual life or lives, and can only be achieved when one desires to focus on that objective. It is accomplished only by delving deep into the inner being via yoga and meditation to achieve the realization that the Self, the Atman, is one with the Supreme, and that all beings are ultimately in union together.

Rather than an outward identity with a particular code of beliefs, Hinduism emphasizes an inner relationship with God. It is experiential. The highest truth is the knowledge that one's Self will become one with the Divine. However, throughout the many lives an individual has, this goal of self-knowledge is often obscured by human desires and the attainment of those desires.

As these cravings are realized and the negative karma that often accompanies their achievement is paid, eventually one's only yearning becomes the return to one's true nature. By liberating the Self from the ignorance and desires of the sensual world including the pursuit of fame, power or wealth, the return to the real home can follow.

With this realization, attention is finally centered on the observances and behaviors that will promote accomplishing this: truthfulness, non-violence, self-control, honesty, no attachments, cleanliness, contentment, self-study, and surrender to the Divine. Furthermore, practices of rituals for the purification of the mind and the promotion of social welfare for all creatures include repeating mantras, meditation for Truth realization, pilgrimages to holy sites, charity to others in need, respect for parents and elders, respect for one's Guru or teacher, study and transmission of teachings, protection of the earth, purity of diet, living with moderation and simplicity, non-interference in other's lives, respect for all beneficial spiritual views and the perpetuation of peace.

Hindu Holidays and Celebrations

Of all the organized religions, Hinduism encompasses the largest number of religious festivals and holidays. Celebrating these festivals and holidays is a major part of social life in Hindu society. Many are local celebrations restricted to certain areas and are typically for a specific god or goddess, which may have a greater significance or influence in specific geographical areas. The following are the major holidays celebrated throughout India. They are listed beginning in January on the western calendar.

Pongal

This is a four-day festival beginning around January 14. It is an agricultural celebration in gratitude for a bountiful harvest. On day one, prayers are said in honor of Lord Indra who provides rain. Traditionally, on this first day, there is a wood or cow-dung fire. All that is old and useless is thrown into the fire—symbolizing beginning the year with a fresh start. On day two, the Sun is honored with rice boiled in milk in an earthen pot as people dressed in traditional clothing sing and dance in praise of the Sun god. On day three, cattle that are used to cultivate the land are honored and often adorned and on the fourth day, Lord Genesha and goddess Parvati are honored.

Vasant Panchami

This holiday celebrates the coming of spring and honors the goddess Saraswati who symbolizes wisdom. This holiday originated during the Aryan era when the Aryan civilization settled initially by the River Saraswati. The goddess Saraswati is celebrated as the goddess of creative energy and of knowledge, language, music, education and all arts. The day is often associated with the beginning of learning or with the reading of books. Yellow is the predominant color for this holiday (from the mustard growing in the fields near the river) and children and adults often enjoy flying kites, dressing in yellow-colored shirts and saris and eating yellow-hued treats.

Maha Shevratri

This is a Hindu festival honoring Lord Shiva. It is observed throughout India and Nepal just before spring. People often fast on the night of Shevratri and Hindu temples are lit and adorned with colorful decorations while people participate in nightlong prayers to Shiva. It is believed that good luck will come into their life after a night of prayer. The biggest celebration occurs in Ujjain where Lord Shiva is believed to have lived. A large procession with an idol of Shiva is held in every city and people gather in the streets to see it pass by.

Holi

This is a celebration of colors and marks the passing of winter and the beginning of spring and summer seasons. Besides several mythological tales associated with this time, it is believed to be a celebration of Radha's undying love for Lord Shiva. There are different intensities of celebration around the country with one festival in Mathura lasting for sixteen days and primarily using flowers. Other places celebrate with colors, water balloons and parties with music and dancing. People greet each other by throwing brightly colored powder. Sweets are also an important part of the festival.

Akshaya Tritiya

A popular holy festival also celebrated by the Jains (in April/May). It's referred to as a golden day because it is believed that anything begun on this day will have good fortune and bring prosperity. It's a favorite day to purchase gold, which in turn will bring more wealth. It is also a popular wedding day. The mythology connected with the day is that during a time of exile, Lord Parasurama presented a bowl named Akshay Tritiya that was never empty and provided unlimited food upon demand. It was also the day when the epic work "the Mahabharata" was written by Vsaya and transcribed by Lord Genesha, the god of Wisdom.

Ratha Yatra

This festival is held in June/July in Puri where over a million pilgrims gather to honor Lord Jagannath, one of the human forms of Lord Krishna. It is a day of equality and integration when all peoples, even those not permitted in the temples, are able to see the deities. Three deities, Lord Jagannath, his brother Lord Balabhadra, and their sister Subhadra, are witnessed by those waiting to see them pass by as they are transported to a large temple in three chariots that are rebuilt each year for the occasion.

Raksha Bandhan

An August celebration honors families and especially the pure and loving relationship between brother and sister. Traditionally a sacred thread is tied around a brother's wrist with a promise of love and affection. The brother, in turn, promises to protect and guide his sister in all that she might encounter. They often exchange gifts on this day.

Krishna Janmashtami

This celebration is in August/September and honors the birthday of Lord Krishna, the most powerful incarnation of Lord Vishnu who was born to rid the world of demons. The day is celebrated with devotional songs, dancing and rituals as well as blowing conchs and rocking the cradle of baby Sri Krishna. Temples and homes are decorated with lights and vigils of prayer are held all night.

Ganesh Chaturthi

Also known as "Vinayaka Chaturthi" this time is for the elephant-headed son of Lord Shiva and Goddess Parvati. He represents wisdom, prosperity and good fortune and this festival is celebrated with much enthusiasm and devotion. Idols of Ganesh are brought into the home for worship during this one to eleven-day celebration. When the festival is over, the idol is carried in a colorful and musical procession and submerged into water. The festival is important for students who worship Ganesh to illuminate their minds. On the Gregorian calendar, this festival takes place in August/September.

Navaratri

In September/October is a ten-day, nine-night festival celebrated with worship and dance. It acknowledges the nine different aspects of Goddess Durga. The theme of the celebration is positivity and ridding oneself of negativity in the forms of hatred, jealousy, anger, greed and violence. It's a celebration of good over evil and one of the legends demonstrates Lord Rama's victory in killing the ten-headed Ravana with the help of Goddess Durga's blessings. This holiday may be celebrated several times in a year.

Diwali or Deepavali

Diwali occurs in October or November and is the most important and famous of all Hindu festivals. It is a "festival of lights" and symbolizes the victory of light over darkness and good over evil. It universally includes the lighting of lamps, lanterns or candles on one's doorstep or window with fireworks and firecrackers to scare off evil spirits. The celebrations honor Lakshmi, the goddess of wealth and prosperity. In different regions of India however, other gods and goddesses may also be worshiped. The celebrations are not only for Hindus but also Jains, Sikhs and Buddhists and each of the five days has a different meaning and reason for celebration.

Day 1 is the birthday of Lakshmi, and in some regions of India, the birthday of Dhanvantari, a wife who saved her husband from death by snakebite by laying out her ornaments to blind and bedazzle the serpent. It can also honor Lord Kubera, the God of assets and wealth. Precious metals like gold and silver are purchased on this day and shops and work places are traditionally decorated and pathways are painted with Rangoli designs with the footprints of Lakshmi to mark her arrival. In villages, cattle and water buffalo are adorned because they represent the main source of a villager's income. Sweets and fruits are offered to Lakshmi on this day. A second legend is that of Rama's exile into the forest, which lasted for fourteen years. His brother and wife Sita joined him. On their return to the city of Ayodha, they were greeted with lighted lamps to guide their return.

Day 2 is a day of remembrance of the killing of the demon Narakasura, an unrighteous being from hell. This day includes a special oil bath (puja) with flowers and sandalwood as part of the ritual. Lord Hanuman is also honored on this day with coconuts, sesame, ghee and other food offerings.

Day 3 is the main celebration with lights everywhere as on this night, Lakshmi, the goddess of wealth, health and fortune, is thought to wander the earth to distribute prosperity everywhere. Mothers are especially honored, and gifts are often exchanged amidst socializing and visiting with friends and relatives. In some areas, Kali replaces Lakshmi as the subject of worship.

Day 4 after Diwali, is a day that is celebrated differently in different areas of India. The day honors the love and devotion between husband and wife and they often exchange gifts to show their dedication to one another.

Day 5 celebrates the bond between brothers and sisters and is exemplified by Lord Krisha and his sister Subhadra. There is gift-giving and food-sharing between brothers and sisters. In different regions, days of honoring between husband and wife or brother and sister may occur on different days than indicated above.

Yatra

This is a pilgrimage of festivals celebrated at different Hindu temples on special, but often different days, once a year. A procession of idols in a chariot, called a *palanquin*, is paraded through the streets for all to see.

References/Bibliography

Ajgaonkar, M.T. (Ed.) (1994). *Mahatma: A golden treasury of wisdom-thoughts & Glimpses of Life.* Mumbai: Hripra Publication.

Bhaskarananda, S. (2002). *The essentials of Hinduism: A comprehensive overview of the world's oldest religion.* (2nd ed.). Seattle: Viveka Press.

Clayton, S.P. & Herxheimer, S. (2010). *Rama and Sita: Path of flames.* London: Frances Lincoln Children's Books.

Easwaran, E. (1985). *The Bhagavad Gita.* Tomales, Calif.: Nilgiri Press.

Easwaran, E. (1985). *The Dhammapada.* Tomales, Calif.: Nilgiri Press.

Easwaran, E. (1985). *The Upanishads.* Tomales, Calif.: Nilgiri Press.

Frawley, D. (2008). *Hinduism, The Eternal Tradition.* New Dehli: Pub. Voice of India.

Hartranft, C. (2003). *The Yogo-Sutra of Patanjali.* Boston & London: Shambhala.

Jayaram V. (Hinduwebsite.com). "Essay Mahabharata." Retrieved February 2, 2017. from http://www.hinduwebssite.com/hinduism/essays/the-origin-and- significance-of-the-epic-mahabharata.asp

Mascaro, J. (1964). *The Upanishads.* London: Penguin Books.

Nathan, R. S. (1989). *Symbolism in Hinduism.* (2nd ed.). Bombay: Central Chinmaya Mission Trust.

Ruhe, P. (2001). *Ghandhi.* New York: Phaidon.

Smith, H. (1991). *The World's Religions.* New York: Harper Collins.

Tejomayananda, S. (1993). *Hindu Culture: An introduction. Mumbai*: Priya Graphics.

Wikipedia contributors. "Hindu festivals." In Wikipedia, The free encyclopedia, Retrieved December 21, 2016, from https://wikipedia.org/wiki/List_of_Hindu_festivals.

BUDDHISM

Hinduism was a part of India's culture for a very long time when Siddhartha Gautama was born in the sixth century B.C. At that time, India's brahmin priests still acted as mediators between man and God. They practiced the Vedic rituals irrespective of the fact that they had little meaning for the common man.

The Upanishads revealed that it was possible to have a direct connection with the Divine through meditation and exploration of the inner self while delving into deeper levels of consciousness. Hindu sages who had experimented with those methods wrote about the techniques in hundreds of accounts. As a result, everyone could access similar experiences and take on the responsibility for their own spirituality using the practices described in the writings of the sages. With the assistance of a teacher (*Upanishad* literally means "to sit at the foot of"), aspirants were guided in the use of meditation as a means to experience the real essence of life that lies beneath the world of an individual's physical being and senses.

The sages who wrote the Upanishads and had themselves discovered their true inner self and its connection with the Divine, were antecedents to the Buddha. Although the Buddha, Siddhartha Gautama, was not the first to obtain enlightenment, he was probably the first to achieve it by his own will and self-determination without the direct assistance of a master or guru.

Prior to the Buddha's accomplishment, only seekers who left society and retired to an ashram or to the forest as dedicated practitioners had any measure of success. The teachings were not widespread nor were they readily available.

In order to pursue and achieve direct experience with the underlying truth and the reality that unites all beings, intense concentration on that which lay beyond the physical senses had to be learned and practiced. Worldly things were considered only temporary or impermanent and therefore ultimately unreal and unimportant.

To develop such concentration, it was required that all human thoughts, emotions, drives, memories, and other such phenomenon associated with the outward personality of an individual be left behind until, at last, there remained only consciousness at the ground level—the Self.

Vedic India considered physical phenomena, human action, and thought to be under the order of a universal natural law or rule termed *dharma* (in Sanskrit). Accepted by the Buddha, the dharma incorporated the concept that even though beings maintain individuality throughout their eons of existence, they are nonetheless interconnected. Furthermore, with the elimination of ego and an attitude of non-self cultivated, there remains the responsibility to do no harm to any living creature. It is from these concepts that the Buddha's teachings came about. In fact, the Buddha's teachings became known *as* the Dharma.

Dharma is best exemplified by the belief that nothing exists or happens by chance nor are happenings predetermined; but they come about through cause and effect. If one causes harm to another through selfish actions, consequences and retribution will result. Likewise, good deeds that produce good effects bring rewards. This is karma—actions good or bad produce effects that are good or bad. There is no role for a divine entity to punish or reward, but rather, it is within one's own control to accumulate positive or negative karma through their actions.

Karma and Rebirth

In Buddhism, as in Hinduism, rebirth is affected by the karma (*kamma*) an individual accrues as they pass through their many life cycles (*samsara*) while utilizing their free will in order to acquire the things and the desires they crave. Karma, which simply means *action*, always has a cause but then becomes an effect.

Depending on the actions one takes, the outcome can be meritorious or detrimental and thereby an individual is responsible for the happiness that karma may bring or the misery that may result. A person's destiny is truly in his or her own hands. Do good and good will come; do evil and reparation must be made sooner or later. One's deeds, words, and thoughts result either in prosperity or failure—happiness or misery. Karma is objective and impersonal. Because Buddhists do not believe in a creator per se, karma is not imposed on an individual by any external agent but, is the result of one's own deeds. It follows then, that karmic law operates on all people regardless of their faith or religion. It's unbiased and explains the inequities that exist for all of mankind who are born into different life situations—happy and prosperous or poor and full of tribulation.

Karma can best be understood in comparison to a bank account. Virtuous and benevolent deeds are deposits into the account of good karma, which ensures a future, or a future life, of trouble-free living. The account must be continually added to so that it does not become depleted or bankrupt. Therefore, good behavior is essential for a good life now *and* in the future in order to maintain happiness.

It should also be mentioned that rebirth into fortunate or unfortunate circumstances can also affect the good or bad karma we acquire. Having plenty certainly makes it easier for a person to be charitable than it would be for someone who has very little. In this situation, generosity in doing good deeds for someone who is poor may outweigh that of only token generosity by a rich man or woman.

Likewise, in threatening situations, a person who acts for the safety or benefit of the group rather than only for himself or his family will certainly be credited with greater positive karma. Victor Frankel, the psychiatrist interred in a Nazi concentration camp, observed that for some, the situation of imprisonment brought out the best of humanity but for others it brought out the worst. Some inmates shared what little food or pleasures they were able to obtain while others hoarded it only for themselves.

Negative karma from one's selfish or regretful acts creates a "debt" that must be repaid. Unpaid karma is not erased when the physical body dies. An opportunity to repay the karmic debt presents itself when the individual is reborn into a situation where he or she can reconcile previous bad actions with good behavior.

An individual does not exist merely for one lifetime, but may have existed for eons changing physical bodies via birth after a previous death. Each rebirth is an opportunity to settle and make reparation for karmic liabilities—an opportunity to modify, to mitigate, and remedy negative karma. Therefore, the circumstance of a rebirth should not be considered as "fate" or destiny.

The Life of the Buddha

The Buddha came, as did Jesus and Muhammad, to teach these truths to large numbers of people. The purpose was not to rebut tradition, but to fulfill its intention by giving physical, worldly meaning to it.

The Buddha sanctioned the teachings of the Upanishads that emphasized direct experience through meditation. He also recognized the importance for people to know first-hand the unity of life and one's ability to determine their own destiny without the need of intervention by another. Where the Upanishad sages wanted "to know", the Buddha wanted "to save" everyone from the sorrow and pain of the physical world.

To answer the question of what is the purpose and goal of life, the sages who preceded the Buddha would have agreed that beyond karmic obligation, the individual personality's drive is to find peace and achieve unity with an indivisible Source.

For the Buddhist, the purpose and goal is to achieve nirvana and liberation from pain and suffering, or, with the actualization of full potential, an "awakening" with the desire to be in service to all other sentient beings. Awakening to the full actualization of Buddhahood enables one to assist others along the pathway to liberation from suffering and samsara.

This goal can be accomplished when the delusion of separateness and selfishness is overcome and there is a realization of the interconnectedness of *all* living things. When one's ego is dissolved and a selfless outlook replaces it, right-living, with compassion and loving kindness towards others, results. Meditation, which was previously only for a few, was taught by the Buddha to all as a means of attaining happiness, health, and the full awakening of nirvana.

The Buddha did not argue with any tradition or faith but gave away India's realized truths of meditation from the Upanishads to anyone who sought to know it—regardless of their position, rich or poor, educated or otherwise. The Buddha's life and teachings exemplified his selfless love for mankind.

Contemporary writing during the Buddha's lifetime was concerned primarily with what he taught after he was "awakened" and enlightened. Rather than a biographical sketch of Siddhartha Gautama's origin, or his travels from place to place, the Buddha's disciples focused on recording his teachings so that they might be preserved when he was no longer physically present. His life was later pieced together and is both interesting and provocative in that a man born in such a favored situation as his might have produced a self-centered, entitled individual rather than one with empathy for those less fortunate and suffering individuals.

The Buddha's Life Story

Siddhartha Gautama was a prince, the son of the King Shuddhodana of Kapilavastu, which is located in today's geography at the border of India and Nepal—now Lumbini (Nepal). The kingdom was located near trade routes leading into the Ganges valley and was therefore quite prosperous. In one of the earliest examples of democracy, King Shuddhodana, Siddhartha's father, shared power with a voting assembly called "the sangha". At the time of Siddhartha's birth, one of several Brahmins commissioned by his father issued a prophecy that his newborn son would either become a great warrior and emperor or would renounce power to become a renowned spiritual leader.

Siddhartha, the name given the baby, literally translated, means "he whose purpose in life has been attained." King Shuddhodana's desire for his son was that he would succeed him as ruler of the kingdom. Therefore, the very gifted boy was given the best education and all that he desired. He was protected by all within the palace from tragedy or any exposure to the sorrows of ordinary worldly life. Because of his sheltered early life, Siddhartha was understandably a sensitive and tenderhearted child.

On one occasion, a cousin shot a swan with an arrow. Siddhartha retrieved the swan and nursed it back to health. When the cousin claimed the bird was his because he'd shot it, Siddhartha asked, "To whom should any creature belong: to him who tries to kill it, or to him who saves it?"

Another time, as a young child during an official ceremony, Siddhartha was left under a rose apple tree for several hours. When the family returned, they found the child still upright and absorbed in a sort of joyous reflection—thought perhaps to be a serendipitous first exposure with meditation. As Siddhartha grew to manhood, he had the best of the best in food and clothing and his life was one of luxury with nothing unpleasant permitted to occur in his presence.

The occasion of his marriage to his cousin Yashodhara provides an illustration of Siddhartha's skill and confidence as a young prince. It is said that Yashodhara was to select a husband via an archery contest. As one of the suitors hit the bull's eye, Siddhartha took his turn confidently and, with his shot, split his rival's arrow in half.

The marriage of Yashodhara and Siddhartha was loving and happy and after some time, the couple had a son who brought them much joy. At twenty-nine years of age however, despite a future that would be filled with everything he might desire, Siddhartha began to question life's purpose and he persuaded his father to allow him outside the palace enclosure.

Although the king agreed, he took every precaution to prevent anything unhappy or negative to occur while the prince traveled along his route outside the palace walls. Soon after departing the palace, however, Siddhartha caught sight of a man suffering from fever and disease. Next, he saw an aged, bent, and wrinkled woman who hobbled along leaning on a staff. Siddhartha questioned his escort and chariot driver Channa, who explained that the first man was diseased and sick, and the hobbling woman was aged and failing. On another venture outside the estate, Siddhartha encountered a corpse stretched out awaiting cremation and it was then that he realized that death would come to all, eventually.

Finally, he encountered a *bhikshu*, one who had left worldly living for the forest to seek that which lies beyond this life. These things caused Siddhartha to ponder all that he had seen, and he was left very disturbed by them.

As a result, his father, sensing his son's unease, arranged for new attempts to provide diversions with entertainment and games for Siddhartha. But even so, his son's thoughts were directed toward the impermanence of life and the underlying question of whether the eventuality of decline and death was all one had to look forward to. These questions weighed on Siddhartha's mind and finally prompted him to leave his family, the protection of the palace, and all that he knew, to venture out into the world in an attempt to understand how to cope with and overcome age, sickness and death.

Worldly Rejection

Before dawn, and accompanied by his charioteer Channa and his beloved horse, the threesome traveled eastward until the break of day, at which time, Siddhartha exchanged his rich clothing and ornaments for saffron yellow rags he found from the graves of executed convicts. From that moment, saffron yellow became an emblematic color of a Buddhist monk. He ordered Channa to return to the palace with his horse and then burned the remainder of his clothes and cut off his long black hair. After that, he owned no more than his robe and a mendicant's bowl in which he ate only what was given to him.

In the forest, Siddhartha studied yoga and meditation with the best teachers he could find, mastering quickly all they had to teach him. But still he found no peace. Next, he met a small group of ascetics (who later became his disciples) and during the six years they spent together, they undertook a life of severe austerity.

Eventually, the developing Buddha reduced his daily intake of food to one grain of rice a day and he became extremely emaciated. In that condition he realized that he no longer had the vitality to concentrate sufficiently to meditate. With his new understanding, when presented with a thanksgiving offering from one who had just bore her first healthy child, he relented, broke his fast and ate. After eating slowly and regaining some strength, the aspiring Buddha lit an oil lamp and set it afloat on the nearby river while declaring that if the lamp floated downstream, he would not attain enlightenment.

At first, the lamp drifted within the eddies of the water, but then it moved in the direction counter to the current. His disciples, who had been so impressed with Siddhartha's unbreakable determination of austerity, witnessed these events and severely chastised him before they left him alone so that they might continue their ascetic way without him. As it was then springtime, Siddhartha somehow remembered the experience years before during springtime when he experienced the joyful, serendipitous meditation as a child under the rose apple tree. He vowed to try and repeat that occurrence. Finding a fig tree near the city of Gaya, he seated himself in the position for meditation and pledged not to leave that spot until he found the way beyond death and decay.

Siddhartha quickly went into a deep, sense-free meditation, only to be visited and tempted by the demon Mara. Similar to the time when Satan tempted Christ before he began his earthly teachings, Mara attempted to derail the aspiring Buddha with false promises and diversions. Mara, the altar ego of every human, provided motives and justification to disrupt his good intentions. Siddhartha overcame every ploy that Mara proposed and at last slipped into a profound stillness where individual distinction dissolves into the interconnectedness with the universe.

When the dawn came at last, the tree under which he sat burst into bloom as if to celebrate that the man once known as Siddhartha was now "the Buddha—the awakened one". He had succeeded in finding that place of freedom, of liberation from sorrow, pain and death—nirvana.

The Buddha might have remained in nirvana; but, with a faint remembrance of others who were left behind, it is said his heart was moved with pity and compassion and he willed himself to lead others to the freedom he had found. The tempter Mara once again argued that the way was too difficult for those immersed in the world of desires and worldly goods. Mara assured him that his mission would be fraught with difficulties and failure. The Buddha considered those words and didn't dispute them, but reasoned that if only a few who desired to end their suffering and sorrow would listen, he would teach them so that they might achieve liberation.

Having made that decision, the Buddha stayed in the same place for several weeks probing deep into all that life entails, including the nature of both sorrow and happiness. He attained nirvana repeatedly during his prolonged meditations until he manifested it every moment—both awake and asleep. Finally, he felt ready to lead others to the freedom he had discovered and had attained permanently.

Buddha, The Teacher (from the Dhammapada)

Like Moses, when he descended Mt. Sinai after speaking with God, and Jesus after his baptism, when the Buddha returned from his sojourn of intense meditation and experiences of nirvana, it was said he had a countenance that shone, and his radiance bedazzled those who saw him. People gathered wherever he was to listen to what he taught as he described nirvana, a state beyond the reach of death or pain or sorrow. He taught all that he had discovered to whoever had an interest, holding nothing back for those who wished to leave behind the sufferings of the world.

His teachings became known as the Dharma and they included the Four Noble Truths. Two of the truths addressed why a person is destined to endure seemingly endless cycles of samsara, and two truths addressed how to overcome and escape from them.

Next, he taught the Eightfold Path, an expansion of the Four Noble Truths, which specified what practices one must do to escape the cycles of birth and death. The Four Noble Truths and the Eightfold Path will be discussed later in more detail.

The Middle Way and Liberation for All

Accordingly, the Buddha proposed that for those seeking spiritual enlightenment, they should put forth the right effort with dedication and constant endeavor. He cautioned that people would be best served to avoid the two extremes of either austere practices of abstinence, or the opposite, indulgent conduct. Rather, he recommended for best success in accomplishing the desired end, a more moderate approach is the way. A calm, peaceful and fruitful existence is the correct mindset to achieve success.

Eventually, during the Buddha's time, the question arose: "Could only men overcome the sufferings of the physical world?" The Buddha responded that every human has the right and the capacity to overcome suffering. This, then, led to the opportunity for women to become part of a spiritual community and to focus on the way of the Buddha in order to achieve their own spiritual liberation.

In addition to the establishment of monasteries for monks to leave behind their worldly responsibilities, desires, and attachments to follow a focused path toward the spiritual goal, women could also follow that example and become nuns in a dedicated spiritual community known as a *sangha*.

Even though the Buddha taught how one might reach the goal of liberation from suffering and nirvana by way of the Eightfold Path, he also advised hopefuls, known as bodhisattvas, who desired enlightenment for the benefit of helping others, to become proficient in analytical meditation. Through meditation, they would be able to achieve satisfactory and convincing answers to their questions rather than submitting to a dogma provided by others.

The Buddha deemed it important that one should be convinced of the Truth rather then rely on another's word. Even though the Buddha taught the way to enlightenment, he also stressed that it is each person's responsibility to strive to answer his or her own questions and/or appease his or her own doubts along the way.

Once convinced, aspirants should be dedicated and steadfast in their endeavor and not allow their purpose to be sidetracked. With love and dedication, spiritual endeavors will never die or fail even in a material world that often seems to forget the importance of the effort to reach the goal of liberation and nirvana.

The Buddha's Later Years

The first of the Buddha's disciples—the same five that had once shunned him when he had abandoned asceticism—immediately realized when they saw his countenance that something extraordinary had occurred. Likewise, those who met Siddhartha for the first time wondered if he was a god or an angel. To that inquiry the Buddha simply replied, "I am awake!"—the literal meaning of the word "buddha".

Next, the disciples wanted to know what he'd found and how they, too, could become "awake". Thus began the Buddha's teachings to whomever wanted to leave behind their selfish intents and follow the path to transcend physical and material desires and achieve liberation and freedom from all pain and suffering.

Once nirvana is obtained, it cannot be lost, and the Buddha might have chosen to remain in that state forever. He vowed, however, as many Buddha's have since, to teach others how to subjugate themselves and leave behind their selfish desires and passions in exchange for liberation from the sufferings that self-centered living inevitably brings.

So, the Buddha set out to teach the dharma—right thought and right action—to those who would listen. He walked from village to village; from city to city his fame and gentle countenance preceded him as he drew crowds wherever he went. Inevitably there were those who wanted to be part of his movement and they joined with him, immediately abandoning their homes and families to become monks.

He eventually returned to his home and his family who had grieved since his departure years before. He was welcomed with open arms and they too, became followers. His father and Rahula, his now-grown son, became monks. The stepmother who had raised him, Mahapajapati, the sister of his birth mother (his mother had died shortly after Siddhartha was born), established the first order of nuns.

For more than forty years the Buddha walked and taught the dharma in north India, teaching others how to escape the sufferings of life by accepting the Four Noble Truths and following the Eightfold Path. The continuing cycles of life after life with the acquiring and canceling of positive or negative karma could be overcome following this path. Only during the monsoons did the Buddha rest until, at the age of eighty, he fell ill. When his faithful monks feared he might leave them, he reassured them they no longer needed him to spread the word. They knew the dharma, they had witnessed it for themselves and they were able to guide others so that the teachings might endure. Shortly thereafter, the Buddha, who became known as

Buddha Shakyamuni, entered parinirvana (nirvana after dying) for a final time.

His face and skin shone, which the Buddha had previously remarked would happen, when one entered complete nirvana (fully awakened) for the first time and for the last.

Continuing the Buddha's Teachings: Two Schools Emerge

The Buddha's teachings were initially orally transmitted, but after a few hundred years, although the basic tenets of the teachings were intact, different interpretations began to emerge. Eventually, it became necessary to preserve the teachings in written form known as the Pali canon. The scriptures were written in sutras or concise statements, often in verse, and they detailed rules for right conduct in living as well as the way to achieve insight and wisdom.

The scriptures were voluminous. In addition to the sutras and comprehensive explanations of their meaning, they also contained Buddha's stories and parables. As a whole, they became the theoretical foundation for teachings in monasteries and convents. A subset of verses known as the Dhammapada, addressed the way or path of the dharma—that of right thought and action. It was concise and most likely recorded first by the Buddha's disciples as a handy, succinct reference meant for those living a normal life outside the monasteries and convents.

The written Pali canon, later also translated into Sanskrit, became the principal ideology for the Theravada school of Buddhism. Although overall there was agreement on the principles and the practice of the Buddha's core dharma teachings, there were different interpretations on monastic rules and other academic points. The original strict Theravada philosophy remained, but the Mahayana school evolved also. As time passed, language and the cultures of countries where Buddhism spread likewise impacted the teachings in minor ways. Of the major concepts however, the two major schools were in agreement:

- Shakyamuni Buddha was their teacher
- The Four Noble Truths and the Eightfold Path were the same
- Dependent Origination (things are caused) was recognized by both
- Both rejected a supreme creator
- Both accepted the concepts of impermanence, suffering, virtuous and moral conduct, no self or emptiness and meditative concentration as a pathway to nirvana with the achievement of wisdom for enlightenment.

Theravada Buddhists followed the orthodox traditions established at the origin of the spreading practice. Mahayanists changed some of the old religious customs in accordance with the countries where Buddhism spread including teaching in the language of the country where the dharma is practiced. The Mahayana philosophy is considered the Middle Way in that it emphasizes relativity between the extremes of nihilism and over-indulgence. Likewise, ascetic means in the achievement of realization is not necessary or recommended, but rather that of a calm, focused pathway.

Theravada Buddhism is practiced in Sri Lanka (the first place it was spread to), Cambodia, Laos, Burma, Thailand, Vietnam, Malaysia, Indonesia, and parts of China.

Mayahana Buddhism dominates in Tibet, Nepal, Bhutan, China, Korea, and Japan. Zen Buddhism of China and Japan evolved to emphasize the importance of the meditative aspect: of looking inward rather than outward as the only way to achieve enlightenment. Moment-to-moment awareness and mindfulness are stressed in Zen Buddhism.

Summary of Core Beliefs of All Buddhists

As previously discussed, there is karmic debt that one has from the recurring cycles of life and death and Buddhists believe that debt is continued with one's consciousness. With each new birth, a person chooses his or her birth situation with the intent to work out that debt and hopefully shift the negative karma to a more positive one. This choice of rebirth may be as an animal for a very large debt or if good karma has been acquired, a person may be born as a god or goddess in which case further opportunity to acquire good karma is possible by helping others.

If it is a human rebirth, a person is endowed with a conscious mind and the freedom of choice. To reach enlightenment, it is the mind that must be controlled as it is the obstacle that continually strives to promote itself. Its natural condition is to crave its own existence and its own desires. Humans become as they think, and the natural thought is toward individualism and self-promotion, which, at its greatest height, can lead to greed, jealousy, and even hate. Recognition of this egocentric tendency has been acknowledged not only by Buddhists, but also by many others, including Freud. In Milton's Book I of *Paradise Lost*, it is written, "The mind is its own place and in itself can make heaven of hell or hell of heaven."

The Buddha prescribed being part of a community (a *sangha*) that encourages following the dharma—the Four Noble Truths and the Eightfold path. A *sangha* provides a haven for like-minded practitioners and it promotes and supports the endeavor to escape from the continuous cycles of birth and death, suffering, disease, and infirmities. Through right meditation, as part of the Eightfold Path, the mind's agenda of self-interest can be overcome as one strives to enter into deeper consciousness where all processes of the mind abate into absolute stillness and tranquility. At this place, the individual self is abandoned and there transpires the realization of emptiness (no self) including the truth regarding the lack of any independent being.

It is then recognized that the purpose of being is to be in union with the love and peaceful existence of the universe as a whole, where individuality and its selfishness are replaced by altruistic compassion and loving-kindness for all.

The Buddha further reminded us that we should not take his word for this, but we should validate it through our own experience. Additionally, he forbade followers to worship him; but rather, he wished to be thought of only as a teacher. It was the teaching that should be revered.

The Four Noble Truths

Basic to all Buddhist pathways are the Four Noble Truths as relayed by the Buddha when he emerged from his awakening meditation and began teaching what he had discovered. These truths are universal and state:

1. All beings desire happiness, but because nothing is permanent all endure suffering, which is caused.

2. The cause is ignorance with continuous craving and grasping for one's selfish desires, which are impermanent.

3. This ignorance and selfishness can be conquered and dispelled by training the mind and freeing it from selfish desires so the joy and peace of nirvana can take its place.

4. To achieve nirvana or full enlightenment (Buddhahood), the eightfold path rids one of selfishness, purifies the mind, and delivers a person from suffering.

To assist in realizing the Four Noble Truths and then following the Eightfold path, the "Three Jewels" are recommended for aspirants. These are: 1) the Buddha, as teacher, who himself became enlightened; 2) the Dharma, which is the Buddha's teachings for achieving this goal; and 3) the Sangha, a community of like-minded aspirants who support one another on the journey towards attaining freedom from suffering.

The Eightfold Path

This pathway is the Buddha's prescription for self-purification in order to achieve liberation from selfish desires and therefore freedom from suffering. Within this path are three components that a devotee must develop: morality, mental concentration, and wisdom. The progress along this pathway varies with the individual as they seek to gain spiritual growth toward liberation; however, constant throughout the process is the adherence to morality and the faithful abstinence from wrong actions and misdeeds. Without these negative behaviors, the mind can maintain control and is enabled to develop concentration and the eventual attainment of wisdom.

The path includes:

1. Right Understanding
2. Right Thought
3. Right Speech
4. Right Action
5. Right Livelihood
6. Right Effort
7. Right Mindfulness
8. Right Concentration

Morality practice is right-speech, which includes not only truthfulness, but also the elimination of slander and gossip. Harshness of speech and controlling another by speech are also factors within this objective. Civil discourse with gentle, truthful words is advocated to bring meaningful harmony by way of kindness.

Right-action entails not only respect for life, but also respect for property and for personal relationships. It includes abstaining from taking life or harming other sentient beings. One should not take what is not theirs through theft, deception, or by other forceful measures. One should honor personal relationships by not committing adultery, avoiding sexual misconduct and maintaining the love and trust of others with the result of making society, as a whole, a better place to live.

Right-livelihood focuses on the manner in which one earns a living. It includes right speech and right action, but also other principles of moral conduct that are devoid of unwholesome sources of revenue such as human trade, trading of weapons, trading in flesh, and trading in intoxicating drinks or drugs. Hunting and fishing for pleasure or for food is also contained within this precept as these activities bring about suffering and harm to other sentient beings.

Mental concentration is a result of right effort, which is the development and practice of a positive, enthusiastic attitude in the way one's life is conducted, including one's career, one's study, or one's practice of the dharma. It includes the rejection of wrong thoughts and unwholesome mental states, which are replaced with the natural state of mind of wholesome thoughts.

Right-mindfulness is developed by continual awareness of the present moment including posture and breathing during meditation. The mind should be clear, attentive, and aware of present surroundings rather than be distracted and clouded.

Right-concentration is developed and perfected by sustained focus and attention on a chosen object without distraction. The intent is to acquire one-pointed awareness of that single object, which may be either physical or mental. This concentration is without distraction or wavering and without anxiousness or drowsiness. The development of this ability leads to well-being, a calm abiding, joy and tranquility. It prepares the mind to be receptive, to gain insight and obtain wisdom as to the true nature of all things (*Vipassana, Sanskrit*).

Wisdom is right understanding or that of knowing and understanding things as they really are, rather than how they may appear. This includes the laws of karma with its merits or demerits and the requirement of reconciliation depending upon the good or bad actions that have accumulated. It includes the comprehension of how negative karma can be eliminated by avoiding evil and by doing good deeds.

Right understanding includes the realization of the Four Noble Truths and the necessity for eradicating ignorance with the cultivation of wisdom and insight in order to understand the truth regarding life and all phenomena.

Right thought (or right aspirations) refers to a mental state void of wrong notions or ideas; but rather that of pure thoughts that lead to liberation from suffering. This is accomplished with a detachment from selfish worldly pleasures and the maintenance of kindness, goodwill and benevolence as well as harmlessness and compassion for all beings. As aspirants progress along their spiritual paths, all ill will and negativity is replaced increasingly with loving-kindness and compassion.

The Six Perfections or Paramitas

The six paramitas (Mahayana Buddhism) are the true nature of an enlightened being and are therefore traits to be cultivated and strived for. They are our own true nature as well, even though they may be obscured by anger, delusion, greed and fear. There are three virtuous perfections and three spiritual ones to practice.

1. Generosity: giving for the benefit of others with an attitude that is sincere and without any expectation of recognition or reward. Work done for others to make one "feel" good is not considered a true generosity paramita.

2. Morality: rendering the best response to all situations with selfless compassion.

3. Patience: enduring personal hardships, tolerance for others and an acceptance of suffering with composure. It is the ability to withstand.

4. Energy and zeal: to render the best effort to obtain enlightenment for oneself and for the benefit of others.

5. Perfecting meditation: cultivating the mind to achieve clarity and insight with single-pointed concentration where all sense of self disappears.

6. Wisdom: realization of emptiness with the understanding that all phenomena are without self-essence or independent existence. This is transcendent knowledge with no self and other, no duality. This state of wisdom is obtained by practicing the other five paramitas.

These are the qualities of a Buddha that develop if practiced diligently with joy and perseverance.

Stages of the Path to Reach Nirvana and Enlightenment

When an aspirant of Buddhism is altruistically motivated by compassion for the sufferings of other beings, the intention (*bodhicitta*) of the practitioner to achieve wisdom and insight in order to save other sentient beings from endless cycles of samsara is desired. Vowing to follow this desire to that of full awakening or Buddhahood, the individual is then known as a *bodhisattva.* It's an arduous journey to undertake for the betterment and elimination of suffering for all sentient beings that may take eons to accomplish.

There are five paths to achieve this:

1. Accumulation

2. Preparation

3. Seeing or Insight

4. Meditation

5. No more learning

When one's compassion for others results in the aspiration to become a bodhisattva and the desire to be awakened, one must not only reconcile karma but also live a life in accordance with the Four Truths and the Eightfold Path for purification of the mind and body. One must accumulate merit by living a selfless life that focuses on always doing what is best for others without regard of any benefit for the seeker of awakening. Cultivating and practicing the Six Paramitas, enhances the accumulation of merit. They emphasize generosity, morality, and patience with energy and zeal, concurrently. It might take eons to accumulate sufficient merit and complete this phase of the enlightenment endeavor.

After sufficient merit has been accumulated, the aspirant next prepares for understanding of the truth of life and the ultimate nature of things. It's a time of reaffirmation and that of pursuing insight and wisdom as an essential element of understanding. This path to insight follows as the truth is realized, even though there may remain obscurations and lack of clarity in the full understanding of the nature of things.

To resolve the final limiting factors before Buddhahood is achieved, the remaining obscurations must be eliminated with the perfection of wisdom, which includes the realization and solidification of no self and the understanding of dependent origination. With these final necessary realizations, the bodhisattva can transcend all limitations to help others realize enlightenment.

The insight and wisdom required to traverse the path to enlightenment is accomplished by meditation. The Buddha relayed to his followers four stages of meditation as part of the Eightfold Path. It's a necessary and important part of the process to obtain wisdom and finally, to acquire nirvana. The technique laid out by the Buddha to his disciples and followers was not all that different from what the Upanishad sages described or from that used by western mystics such as John of the Cross, Teresa of Avila, Augustine or Meister Eckhart.

The method is of universal application not at all exclusive to Buddhism; it requires extreme dedication and fortitude to break through the superficial consciousness to experience the center of man's being. It takes determined effort and years of trial and practice. It requires courage, resilience, and an unwavering will.

Profound meditation (dhyana) has *four phases*. In the initial meditation experience, because of a person's lifetime dependence on the physical senses and the constant stimuli that vie for attention, the mind is easily distracted and unable to concentrate for more than a few seconds at a time. Eventually however, under the right circumstances, it is possible to achieve focus, leaving behind sensory input to move inward for the purpose of contemplation. Persons, on such an occasion, may not be aware of others around them or even hear conversations. This is the first level of meditation and to sustain this state of inward concentration for even a short period of time without awareness of the outside world is an accomplishment and is beneficial so that one may calmly reflect on deeper causes and their actions. This, in itself, can be life altering.

The second phase of dhyana: As concentration deepens and the distractions from the outside are successfully curtailed, eventually ego and self-interest can also be put aside and replaced with the desire for the betterment of the whole of mankind. This may take a very long time to achieve, as one must slowly descend into the subconscious to examine what lies there. Ultimately during this phase of one-point concentration, processes of the mind slow to the point that they are brought under control so that thoughts and feelings can be thoroughly examined. One sees more clearly without the entanglement of emotions. In this depth of consciousness, neither the sense world nor one's personal identity is of concern. One's body, one's thoughts, feelings and personal desires are eliminated. It is the inner world—deep within our unconscious—that has been found and entered.

The third phase of dhyana: Thought, having been sufficiently slowed to enable selfless examination of the issues of humanity, will eventually stop entirely and the meditator can glimpse for an instant into the deeper internal consciousness. This is an intense experience, called *Bodhi*, that is a momentary insight—a glimpse into pure light and joy. At this level, the insight is brief but the knowledge of this state of being is so intense that one's only desire is to stop the mind again and repeat this intensely exalting experience.

All of life's lesser desires dissipate and there remains only the longing to reestablish this insight; then, the joy of this state becomes life's goal. Only a thin veil of separateness remains, which continues to isolate one despite any amount of will and drive to overcome it. This barrier, however, cannot be crossed permanently until the accounts of karma are cleared either by deeds of merit or karmic payback.

Although the wait at this threshold is frustrating and may continue for months or years, at some point, with perseverance, time will stop along with the mind and the intense joy to which the body and nervous system respond will flood the consciousness with the realization that one is no longer a separate creature or a finite being, but inseparable from the whole of creation with the responsibility to serve all of life. This situation, however, is not yet permanent.

The fourth dhyana: During this final phase, the meditator revisits this realm over and over and the experience of unity is realized again and again. At all times there is a continual awareness of unity with one always "awake" to this. This is nirvana where the phenomenon of separateness is extinguished. When one returns to consciousness and a personality may seem to reappear, the person has been forever changed—one is no longer separate but is in unity with love and all of life. In this exalted state *samsara* can cease, the purpose of life has been achieved and the current physical body is the last—unless—as the Buddha did, one chooses to assist others to achieve this goal and to continue in a physical life to accomplish this—the most compassionate of altruistic desires.

The word "nirvana" literally implies a blowing out or extinguishing of self-will and self-passion to become one with all of life. A unity with all life is created with the absence of fault or imperfections. The attainment of perfection is one's true nature and is what remains after self-centeredness is eradicated. It is only the conscious mind with its ego that interferes with the unity of the soul and the supreme love that is all-inclusive.

Practice of Tantras — An Additional Path to Enlightenment

By means of meditation aimed for insight and wisdom, a bodhisattva is on the traditional pathway to achieve enlightenment. This may take years or even eons. Alternatively, an esoteric belief system, *Vajrayana*, termed the thunderbolt or diamond method, is the practice of *tantra*, which provides an additional expedited way to enable enlightenment within a single lifetime.

The aspirant begins by using traditional practices of insight meditation and perfected virtues of charity, patience and wisdom; however, other techniques carefully guided by a teacher, are also used. Prior to practicing Vajrayana techniques, vows of the bodhisattva must be taken and empowerment must be formally granted.

Practices may involve repeating mantras, use of mandalas (intricate artistic designs using colored sand, which upon completion are destroyed to emphasize the impermanence of all things) and visualization exercises with a deity. A representation of the deity, a statute or painting is used along with various rituals.

The aspirant transfers his mind by imagery and visualization to the deity in order to acquire the qualities that the deity possesses, including the wisdom of emptiness (no self) and the conjoining with the universal mind. There is a great deal of secrecy with tantric practices between student and teacher so as to allow only those with a dedicated and serious intent to use the techniques. The female goddess Tara, with her many aspects and virtuous qualities, is often used in Vajrayana tantric practice.

Dependent Origination (no creator)

This important Buddhist perspective expands and elaborates the meaning of the Four Noble Truths and it delves into the explanation for samsara—the continuous cycle of birth and death with its concomitant suffering. It is represented by a wheel of life with twelve divisions that roll along cycle after cycle—rebirth after rebirth. The goal is to bring an end to the cycles of this wheel and obtain liberation from the suffering the cycles cause.

The proposition of this theory is that phenomena are caused by previous happenings (a precursor cause); it becomes the effect from a previous cause. Excluded from this law is the creation of the universe or the first cause. (The first cause is eliminated because all causes result from an effect but, in this case, there would be nothing to cause an effect.)

A simple explanation of this is that nothing can arise on its own independently, but rather all things are dependent upon a prior cause. As a simple example—the effect of weather: clouds cause rain, rain causes a slippery walkway, a man slips and falls, his leg is broken, he misses work etc. etc.

This Buddhist doctrine of dependent origination accounts for the cause of ignorance that affects one's actions and the accumulation of negative karma, which then leads to suffering and endless cycles of existence. The twelve divisions of this wheel illustrate how this occurs:

1 & 2) Because of ignorance, desires and intentional activities arise or possibly are left over from a previous cycle of existence.

3. Desires and intentional activities leave an imprint on consciousness and become part of consciousness.

4. Consciousness formulates the want of mental and physical phenomena.

5. Mental and physical phenomena gives rise to six faculties (five senses and mind).

6. Through these faculties, a connection with mental or physical phenomena occurs.

7. Through this sensual contact, feeling arises.

8. Feeling then becomes a craving, a "thirst" for this mental or physical object.

9. Craving then leads to clinging and grasping to achieve or maintain the desired.

10. Through clinging and grasping, the process of becoming arises.

11. Becoming arises to birth or rebirth.

12. Birth leads to sorrow, pain, grief, despair, aging and death.

To summarize and explain this succession of events further, ignorant causes from a previous life (not knowing the truth) are the precursors for the current birth. Desired activity/actions prevail because of one's misconception (ignorance) that it is these activities and actions that bring one pleasure and fulfillment when in actuality they cause suffering with a result of rebirth after rebirth.

At rebirth, the previous life's consciousness is transferred (including its desires, activities and actions) that now manifest as renewed mental and physical phenomena. With the development of mind and sense contact, sensory experience in the form of seeing, smelling, taste, body sensation, etc. occur, followed by craving, then grasping to possess.

This volition to have or to own might further be accompanied by greed and even hatred. The life of desiring, craving and grasping one thing after another is a mind-body process and it occurs again and again leading to rebirth and more suffering in endless cycles that generate in addition to desire, disease, sorrow, pain, suffering and eventual death.

Humanity, endowed with senses, develops feelings in the mind that quite naturally lead to obtaining physical or mental things. However, it is at this point that the chain of events might be interrupted by way of awareness and wisdom, so that this ignorance might be eradicated. Rather than the intense desire to have or possess, one should be mindful, letting go and detaching from the conditioned continuous desires that are always present.

When there is no longer craving and grasping, there is no longer a need for becoming, for rebirth, for suffering, old age or death. At that point, one becomes free from these physical struggles.

Emptiness

Associated with dependent origination, is the concept of emptiness that proposes that because all phenomena, including all creatures, originate from a previous cause, they are inherently lacking independent existence. This is not to suggest nihilism, but rather that all things are effects of something before and not actually created independently in their current form or manifestation. Although tables, and cars, and people, and all objects exist conventionally—they can be seen and touched—they are reducible to some previous form and not valid as an independent creation.

They have not come about from a creator or of their own volition. They are empty of inherent reality.

Although conventional sources of knowledge, for example, our senses, provide reliable information from the people, objects, and phenomena in the world around us, we are most likely deceived into thinking that these things arise independently on their own.

Buddhism proposes that this is a fallacy. Everything is an effect from a previous cause and therefore the choices an individual makes in response to others' actions or happenings (causes) can change (effect) the course of future events.

Emptiness reinforces the negation of predestination as everything that happens is by *our* own hands or an effect of *our* own choices. It's through this realization that one eradicates ignorance by not only understanding that one's actions determine immediate situational outcomes, but that there may be future ramifications of one's actions as well (karma). This, therefore, requires accurate perception and reasoning of all happenings based on one's developed wisdom, including insight into the actions of others. When one understands that all phenomena are empty and that the actions of others and their interactions are caused, one can better deal with negative behaviors in a more compassionate manner.

Buddhist Belief About a Soul

Rather than a soul that is permanent and endures for eternity, Buddhists believe in a *consciousness*, which is not permanent but continually changes and hopefully evolves. The origin of this consciousness is from eternity and it has been continually reborn after dying from life cycle after life cycle when one has cravings for one thing after another.

According to one's actions in fulfilling those desires, good or bad karma is collected and must be reckoned with and reconciled by fortunate or less-fortunate rebirths. As the physical body wears out, it's this impermanent, always-changing consciousness that leaves the old "container" and enters into a new body to be born again with the continuance of this stream of consciousness.

Buddhists believe this happens ordinarily without a gap i.e. the old body dies and the consciousness immediately enters into a newborn child still in the womb. If there is time between the death of one body and the occupation of another, an intermediate waiting period termed *bardo* occurs. Although the body may be gone, desire for sensual pleasures, craving and grasping continue with this consciousness, giving rise to ceaseless rounds of rebirth, death and fortunate or unfortunate rebirth according to one's karma account.

As has been discussed, to break this cycle of chasing sensual desires, one must destroy all desires of lower personal pleasures and selfishness and overcome the ignorance that has caused them. By following the Four Noble Truths, the Eightfold Path and guided by the Six Paramitas, ignorance is banished, truth is realized, and sorrow removed.

Through the practice of altruism and right-conduct, and by gaining wisdom through meditation, ignorance is extinguished allowing one to leave behind all desires and suffering. One is then liberated from the cycles of death and rebirth, and able to enter nirvana, a state of peace and freedom.

Nirvana or Enlightenment, the Goal

Nirvana is happiness and the leaving behind of suffering caused by ignorance. The accomplishment of nirvana is the personal responsibility of each person. It's the liberation from suffering caused by ignorance and misconception, which will then eliminate the need for endless cycles of rebirth, suffering and death for an individual.

An egoless, selfless attitude with the adoption of compassion and loving kindness in response to another's negative behaviors and actions, rather than the ignorant attitude of retribution, will result in the end of suffering with the additional effect that any negative action has also been weakened.

If an individual is further motivated by compassion to become fully enlightened and to acquire Buddhahood with the intention of helping all sentient beings to also acquire liberation, this noble option is also a choice.

The pathway leading to these outcomes is that of morality, concentration and the development of wisdom, which are inclusive within the Eightfold Path. Concentration and wisdom are further achieved through the four stages of meditation as part of the process of the Five-step Path to enlightenment, as described earlier. Following these paths is essential to gain the wisdom necessary to eventually achieve freedom from ignorance and its accompanying cravings.

Wisdom is a true understanding of the nature of things; and its development first requires quieting the mind so that focused contemplation can occur. Meditating on the temporary nature of worldly pleasures should have the effect of weakening the strong desire to pursue them. Meditating on loving-kindness and compassion lessens dislike or the desire to harm others so that instead of rendering feelings of envy and jealousy, one rejoices over another's good fortune and prosperity. The result of such practice is the extinction of hatred, ignorance and delusion. When one eliminates these traits and realizes the interconnectedness of all things, loving-kindness, peace and tranquility, void of pain and suffering, is the result.

References/Bibliography

BBC – Religions. (2009). "Buddhism at a glance". Retrieved on December 29, 2018 from www.bbc.co.uk/religion/religionsbuddhism/ataglance/glance/shtml.

Armstrong, K. (2001). *Buddha*. Penguin lives series. New York: Penguin Putman.

Chodron, T. (2005). *How to free your mind: Tara the liberator*. Itheca, N.Y. and Boulder, CO.: Snow Lion Publication.

Easwaran, E. (1985). *The Dhammapada*. Tomales, Calif.: Nilgiri Press.

Garfield, J. L. (1995). *The fundamental wisdom of the middle way*. N.Y., Oxford: Oxford University Press.

Goldstein, J. (2017). "Dependent-origination". Retrieved July 3, 2017, from https://tricycle.org/magazine/dependent-origination/

Gyatso, T. (1995). *The world of Tibetan Buddhism*. Boston: Wisdom Publications.

Gyatso, T. (1992). *The meaning of life from a Buddhist perspective*. Boston: Wisdom Publications.

Gyatso, T. (2001). *Stages of meditation*. Itheca, N.Y.: Snow Lion Publications.

Hanh, T. N. (1991). *Old path white clouds: Walking in the footsteps of the Buddha*. Berkeley: Parallax Press.

Kongtrul, D. (2006). *Its Up to You: The practice of self-reflection on the Buddhist path*. Shambhala, Boston & London, 2006.

Kornfield, J. (2011). *The Buddha is still teaching: Contemporary Buddhist wisdom*. Boston and London: Shambhala.

Newland, G. (2008). *Introduction to emptiness as taught by Tsong-kha-pa's Great Treatise on the stages of the path*. Itheca, N.Y.: Snow Lion Publication.

Scott, D. & Doubleday, T. (1997). *The elements of Zen*. N. Y.: Barnes & Nobles Books.

Smith, H. (1991). *The World's Religions*. N. Y.: HarperCollins.

Suzuki, S. (1983). *Zen mind, beginner's mind: Informal talks on Zen meditation and practice*. N.Y. and Tokyo: Weatherhill.

Watts, A. (1989). *The way of Zen*. N.Y.: Vintage Books.

Buddha Dharma Education Association & BuddhaNet. (2008). "The Vajrayana: The Thunderbolt vehicle". Retrieved June 27, 2017, from http:// Desktop/Buddhist%20Schools:%20Vajrayana %20 (Tibetan).webarchive.

Buddha Dharma Education Association & BuddhaNet. (2008). "Theravada & Mahayana". Retrieved June 27, 2017, from http:// www.buddhanet.net/e- learning/buddhistworld/schoolsl.htm

Dhammananda Maha Thera (BuddhaSasana). "The noble eight-fold path – the middle way". Retrieved on June 27, 2017, from http://www.budsas.org/ebud/whatbudbeliev/78.htm.

Dhammananda Maha Thera (BuddhaSasana). "Mind and matter (Nama-Rupa)". Retrieved on June 27, 2017, from http://www.budsas.org/ebud/whatbudbeliev/73.htm.

Dhammananda Maha Thera (BuddhaSasana). "Tri-Pitaka". Retrieved on June 27, 2017, from http://www.budsas.org/ebud/whatbudbeliev/62.htm.

Dhammananda Maha Thera (BuddhaSasana). "Two main schools of Buddhism". Retrieved on June 27, 2017, from http://www.budsas.org/ebud/whatbudbeliev/59.htm

Dhammananda Maha Thera (BuddhaSasana). "Rebirth". Retrieved on June 27, 2017, from http://www.budsas.org/ebud/whatbudbeliev/96.htm

Dhammananda Maha Thera (BuddhaSasana). "Law of dependent origination". Retrieved on June 27, 2017, from http://www.budsas.org/ebud/whatbudbeliev/106.htm

Dhammanananda Maha Thera (BuddhaSasana). "What is Kamma"? Retrieved on June 27, 2017, from http://www.budsas.org/ebud/whatbudbeliev/87.htm

Wikipedia contributors. "Visuddhimagga". In Wikipedia, The free encyclopedia, Retrieved June 27, 2017, from https://wikipedia.org/wiki/Visuddhimagga#Seven_Stages_of_Purification

Wikipedia contributors. "Vipassana". In Wikipedia, The free encyclopedia, Retrieved June 27, 2017, from https://wikipedia.org/wiki/Vipassana

GOING FORWARD

The Abrahamic religions—Jewish, Christian and Muslim—have evolved over time for different peoples according to their way of life and often their geographical location.

The common element is that all three religions believe in the same God/Allah but their different circumstances produced separate scriptures that parallel their individual situations. If we are religious followers of one of these three systems of belief, perhaps we would be better served to think, realize, and acknowledge the legitimate right of others to believe in accordance to their own heritage.

If humanity is indeed created in the image of God, as these three religions avow, being made in God's image certainly does not refer to the *appearance* of an unseen God, but rather to the *behavior* of an unseen God i.e. that of being loving and accepting of all His people, along with their differences. Would it be possible to recognize Jesus or Muhammad today if they physically walked in our presence? Muhammad, who is never portrayed by any sort of image, would indeed be difficult to visualize. Jesus, on the other hand, typically appears as a blue-eyed, fair-skinned fellow who, in reality, was an ostracized Middle Eastern, olive-skinned, Jewish man.

St. Augustine was dark-skinned and born in present day Morocco, yet he is portrayed mostly as Caucasian. We are more comfortable, it seems, to visualize our ideals, our heroes, our prophets and perhaps our God as looking like us so we can better relate. Yet, it is noteworthy that humans, all humans, regardless of their ethnicity and physical characteristics, are said to be "in the image of God". The acceptance of this fact–that all people regardless of race, nationality, gender or religion are created in the image of God–may be our ultimate challenge, our greatest hurdle to comprehend, realize, and accept.

Maybe it is the definitive purpose of our earthly existence: to learn how to live with one another peacefully with mutual respect; to understand and accept each other regardless of where we have come from or how we perceive and worship our God.

Can we find a way to accept that the cultural or historical lens with which others view their world affects and molds their unique beliefs that are equally real and relevant to them as our beliefs and behaviors are to us? Why is it our assumption that if they do not believe our way, they are wrong? The Hindus have stated, "One Source, but many pathways to that Source", which seems to say we all have the right to choose our own way.

If we can accept that viewpoint, once again Mahatma Gandhi's statement provides clear direction: "*We* must become the change we want to see in the world–it doesn't occur by bullying or by forcing our way on others. If we can change ourselves (by exhibiting more tolerance for others), we can one by one change the world."

Henrik Edberg (2013), a Swedish writer and blogger, further expands Gandhi's tip for changing the world by adding 10 rules also derived from Gandhi. They are:

1. Change yourself. If we all changed our tolerance and respect for others' beliefs, the world itself would gradually be changed.

2. You are in control. Only you choose how you think, what emotions you feel and release and how you react to any situation.

3. Forgive and let it go. Don't hold a grudge or be vindictive.

4. Without action nothing can be achieved. Talk alone will most likely not accomplish what needs to be done. Put into practice your beliefs.

5. Take care of this moment. The past is over, the future not yet here. Action is only applicable to this particular time.

6. Remember that everyone is human. Humans make mistakes so avoid beating others up for the mistakes they have made. That includes beating one's self for the mistakes previously made.

7. Persist. Don't give up as success seldom is achieved on the first attempt. (WD-40 a household lubricant is an example of this rule. Thirty-nine previous attempts to develop this product failed. On the fortieth trial, WD-40 was perfected.)

8. See the good in people and help them. Focus on the positive things you observe in others to motivate yourself to be of service to them. In turn this will hopefully inspire them to do the same.

9. Be congruent, authentic, be your true self. Behave and communicate with words that are honest, but kind in both tone

and body demeanor. Avoid phoniness or condescending thoughts, words or actions.

10. Continue to grow and evolve. There is always opportunity to gain deeper understanding of yourself and the world.

Let me try and illustrate that changing our own attitude is the key to a successful outcome with an incident that happened when my daughter played middle school soccer. Because I had a short meeting scheduled before her game, I arranged for her to go with a friend to the soccer field with the intent of being there myself shortly after the start of the game. Being unfamiliar with that particular field, I walked over to one set of bleachers and sat down.

I soon realized I had picked the wrong side and was with parents from the opposing team. I knew this because of very negative remarks and insults that were yelled out when our team made either a good or bad play while they cheered fervently for their own team. Initially my blood pressure began to rise and I was shocked by the harshness of the parents' continued verbal abuse. I decided rather than getting angrier, I would try to change their demeanor by my own actions.

I cheered for our team and garnered some rather stern glances in my direction. Then their team made some good plays and I cheered in appreciation for those plays. When one girl scored a goal or saved a goal, I yelled "great play!" Finally, at half time, we even began a conversation and pointed out our respective daughters.

By the end of the game, which they won, we congratulated each other on a game well played by both sides. It was a total change in conduct from when I first arrived. We both, it seems, had a change of heart.

In terms of religious beliefs, respecting another's beliefs extends to their manner of dress, their holy books and scriptures as well as their way of worship. It follows that if another's belief is not to portray an image of their prophet, as Islam commands for the depiction of Muhammad, it should be respected even if it makes no sense to us. Blatantly disregarding such a belief and ridiculing it by publishing cartoons that make fun of Muhammad demonstrates both a lack of understanding for another's beliefs and complete disrespect for those persons who hold that belief to be important.

As we know, furious, inappropriate reactions often occur by those who have been offended, while the offenders are also outraged because their freedom of speech has been violated. Such was the case with a cartoon published by the French satirical news magazine, *Charlie Hebdo*, and the murderous Muslim overreaction that followed the insult of that publication. Neither action showed tolerance. One displayed ignorance and disregard for the beliefs of another (under the guise of freedom of speech) while the offended other retaliated with an overreaction of violent revenge.

How much better could it have been to dispel that ignorance with the recognition of "a teachable moment" and an explanation of the hurtfulness of such a cartoon—to disavow it with reason and fact rather than revenge. To kill another in revenge is *not* part of Islam as revealed by God in the Quran.

Would the publishers have responded to an explanation of the insult this publication caused and issued an apology? Who knows?

There was a choice on both sides: to disrespect and offend or to respect the diversity of others and their beliefs; to react with restraint with an attempt to dispel the ignorance of the insult or to react with violence?

Unfortunately, with this case, both sides failed. The same can be said for desecrating the scriptures of another's faith or demanding that others dress as we do or want them to (speaking of the hijab). Do we tell a priest not to wear a collar or a monk not to wear a robe?

In the Abrahamic religions, the proclamation of being a "chosen" people is claimed within all three faiths. The Jews were the first to be described as "chosen", when God said to the Israelites: "I am your God and you are my people." They, as a people, have been subjected to slavery and rescued by God and were ultimately scattered throughout the world, ostracized and abused. They suffered immensely during the holocaust, yet were finally able to return to their holy, God-given land to be threatened again today by Iran. It does seem that a loving God has protected the oft-threatened Jewish survival. But, is their being "chosen" meant to be to the exclusion of others who occupy land near them? It is said that God loves all people; and they, too, are in his image.

Jesus, the cornerstone of Christianity, was a Jew and therefore salvation though Jesus might be considered Jewish as Jesus was sent to clarify and teach Mosaic Law. He taught about anger, adultery, divorce, vows, revenge, enemies, charity, prayer, fasting, riches, possessions, judging others, the "narrow gate", the golden rule, the tree and the fruit, the wise and the foolish, the humbleness and innocence like that of a child. And, he initiated a New Covenant from a compassionate, inclusive God and further expanded the "chosen" to include the non-Jews (the Gentiles).

Lastly "chosen", were the "peoples of the desert", who originated from Ishmael, the son of Abraham and Hagar, and who languished in the desert in separate tribal enclaves, each seeking power and riches for themselves without consideration for others. For those peoples, God's plan was through his chosen Muhammad in a context that would be meaningful for them. The Quran was revealed to Muhammad and as Jesus had before him, Muhammad provided an example in the context of the desert people. Given their culture and experience, he taught how those who follow the Quran should live and treat one another with love, respect and reverence to Allah.

As with Moses and Jesus, and then Muhammad, people strayed from the original intent of their teachings after the prophets had gone. It is important to emphasize once again that "chosen" does not mean that the "other" is excluded. In the Muslim Quran, Surah 2: 136, plainly states: "We believe in God, and the revelations given to us, and to Abraham, Ishmael, Isaac, Jacob and the Tribes (Jews), and that given Moses and Jesus, and that given to (all) Prophets from their Lord: we make no difference between one and another of them: and we bow to God (in Islam)."

In Surah 5: 48, it is also revealed: "to you We sent the Scripture in truth, confirming the scriptures (Jewish and Christian) that came before, and guarding it in safety: so judge between them by what God has revealed, and do not follow vain desires, diverging from the truth that has come to you. To each among you, We have prescribed a Law and an Open Way. If God had so willed, He would have made you a single people, but (His Plan is) to test you in what He has given you: so strive as in a race in all virtues. The goal of you all is to God; it is He that will show you the truth of the matters in which you dispute."

So there it is! God's plan plainly revealed in the Quran—his final revelation. There are different ways to know God for different peoples, as planned by God himself, and knowing God is the destination we should all strive for.

From the Eastern religions comes the beautiful, all-encompassing belief that ALL people will eventually know that only God or the love that God represents is real and infinite. For some, God IS the spirit of righteous love that lacks any sort of physicality. ALL peoples will learn sooner or later that the importance of worldly desires such as wealth and power will eventually deplete. Ultimately, the feeling that we lack something we can't identify, and with a building home-sickness felt within the core of our being, within our very soul, sooner or later, we will understand not only the cause of that feeling, but, the remedy. This self-realization will solidify that our most important accomplishment and goal will be the acknowledgement that peace and loving-kindness is what we really seek. By whatever manner, whatever path, whatever belief system we embrace in finding our way, be it Abrahamic or Hindu, Buddhist or other, it matters little as long as we eventually arrive at the destination where love and peace prevail for all people equally and infinitely.

Individuals who have had near-death experiences due to some accident or medical mishap, become aware that their consciousness has left their body and escaped the physical realm. During such an occurrence one is able to see their physical body as a separate entity (from their consciousness itself). Accompanying this separation, the individual typically experiences a remarkable loving peacefulness; a calm abiding where one wishes to remain yet is told they must return to the physical world, as ones' earthly purpose has not been accomplished. Many who have had a near-death experience report feelings of connectedness and unity with all beings. This temporary experience does not belong exclusively to any one system of belief but has been reported in every religion, including the eastern religions, and from ancient times as well.

Although this book is about religion, it is not meant to be a religious book. Its intent is not meant to convince the reader that one faith is better than the other or to convince the atheist that to believe in God is the only way for a sane person to live. In that regard, we should acknowledge that religion itself is not a requirement to be a good person and that the person who finds it difficult to believe in a God may be more honest than the person that is recognized as religious, but whose commitment is lacking and insincere. The intent of this book is rather to inform and explain, to dispel ignorance (lack of knowledge) and to educate about what those who practice any of the five major religions I have described, believe. It is meant to show the commonalities and connections of all religions as well as the evolution of each system of belief in order to explain how and why they have evolved into what they are today. I've suggested and argued that, if there is indeed a God who has created all mankind in his own image as the Abrahamic religions maintain and if that God has given us free will to make choices, the choices of tolerance and kindness should not be only toward those who are like us, but, toward all people, who are also said to be in God's image by the mere fact that they are human.

Recall that in the Quran, Allah revealed his plan: ... "If God had so willed, He would have made you a single people, but (His Plan is) to test you in what He has given you: so strive as in a race in all virtues. The goal of you all is to God; it is He that will show you the truth of the matters in which you dispute."

It should now be apparent that within each system of religious or spiritual belief, a person's vision and interpretation of God is meaningful to them in light of both their ability to comprehend as well as their cultural origin. It is noteworthy that all religions have a version of the Golden Rule as a key tenet. "Do unto others as you would have others do unto you". "Do not do to others what you wouldn't want done to you". With this simple ubiquitous concept, elegant in its simplicity, theft, murder, adultery, false witness, the coveting of another's possessions and in general, a lack of respect for the other, would clearly cease to be. Whether it is the Noahic code, the Ten Commandments, the Hindu lessons from the Bhagavad Gita or the Buddhist Paramitas, all lead to the same directive: that of living a pure life and having an attitude of selflessness while respecting ones fellow man.

No religion advocates violence; if it seems so, it is not being practiced correctly. As in the Bhagavad Gita however, if others (even nations) act or react out of greed or lust for power, action is justified in order to curtail wrong behavior so that greed for wealth or the desire for supremacy does not prevail. It is man's duty to disallow the strong and overly ambitious to trample the weak. It is, with certainty, our duty to prevent and eradicate such behavior, but it must be with the intent of righteousness or justice rather than self-service.

Rather than consider diversity of religious belief, including the absence of religious belief, as something that is divisive and to be disdained, a change of heart and the recognition that the sum of all that can be learned from their differences may indeed lead to a greater understanding of life's purpose. Truly the whole might be greater than the sum of its individual parts!

Hemingway's words in *For Whom the Bell Tolls* are particularly poignant: "Today is only one day in all the days that will ever be. But what will happen in the other days that ever come, can depend on what you do today."

Should we appreciate diversity of religion for its potential to unite us rather than divide us or continue the attitude that only our version of things must prevail?

References and Bibliography

Edberg, H. (2013). "Gandhi's 10 rules for changing the world". Retrieved on March 23, 2019. from DailyGood.com.

Hemmingway, E. M. (1995 reprint). *For whom the bells toll.* New York: Scribner.

Hemmingway, E. M. (n.d.) Retrieved from https://www.goodreads.com.

NOTES FOR DISCUSSION

I would be remiss if I did not suggest things for the reader to consider after acknowledging that a change of heart and attitude in our respect for others is needed. First and foremost is:

1. Seek facts. Seek truth. Do not get your "facts" or your opinions from social media or your friends who may get it from their friends who get it from another rogue source. Keep in mind while seeking facts, that the mission for some so-called "news media" is often not objective news reporting, but rather primarily for the advancement of a particular political outlook or viewpoint. Often assertions are skewed or incompletely reported to create a belief or conclusion in the minds of their viewers and audience to advance a certain agenda. So it is with religious beliefs. Go to the source; read the source itself: the Torah, the Bible's New Testament, the Quran, the Bhagavad Gita, Buddhist philosophy.

2. Whether conservative or liberal in politics, religion, or social behavior, make it a point to listen to the perspective and stance of others. Read and listen to their arguments. You don't have to agree but perhaps you will gain better insight and understanding—even perhaps modify your views.

3. Exercise your right and obligation to express your informed, factual opinion of the facts that you know to be true.

Expressing ourselves respectfully is more powerful than doing so by forceful, abusive language. Exercise your right to vote with informed knowledge. Read newspaper editorials from a variety of different news media. You should be well informed on all sides of an issue. Read opinions contrary to your own beliefs to gain a different perspective.

4. Rather than retaliation against those with whom you dis-agree, think of peacefully sharing viewpoints with the aim of dispelling misinformation and destructive points of view. Attempt to understand why others think as they do.

5. Look for compromise. You do not have to compromise your principles or change your beliefs, but you should demon-strate respect and tolerance for other's opinions with the goal of fruitful, enlightening dialogue. Perhaps you might even alter how you perceive things by engaging with another.

6. Be kind to one another. Practice civil discourse. Practice tolerance and compassion when you disagree.

His Holiness the Dali Lama stated: "Our prime purpose in this life is to help others. And, if we can't help them, at least don't hurt them." How do you feel about that? What ways can you think of to encourage respect and diffuse the angry rhetoric of today's world.

"There is nothing noble in being superior to your fellow man; true nobility is being superior to your former self."

Ernest Hemingway

Please read again pages 10-16 on the steps for the development of compassion in our daily life.

I have attempted to relay as accurately as possible the concepts and beliefs of practitioners of the religions outlined in this narrative in order to promote better understanding of one another's beliefs. If I have portrayed anything erroneous or imprecise, please forgive and inform me through my author's website: lreynoldsandiric.com.